"*Time* is a stunning and poignant story of the power of love and family in a time when the whole world is against you. It's the story of a man desperate to get back to his family, and a woman and children who refuse to give up on him. It's an awe-inspiring story of perseverance and what it means to be a Black family in America—the joy, the sorrow, the victories, and the hurt all in one. Fox and Rob's devotion to each other, their children, and the truth is nothing short of astounding.

Exposing the toll that the American prison system takes on an individual and their family, Fox and Rob's story of heartbreak and perseverance needs to be heard around the world. It's a devastatingly real look into what spawned the couple's mission to abolish mass incarceration. Fox and Rob have already proven their story is one for a generation, but now they've proven their literary prowess as well."

Kenya Barris, writer, producer, director, actor

"This story has to be told. This book has to be read. It's so incredibly perfect for the times we live in—bad personal decisions, misplaced accountability, genuine redemption, and eventually dignity and justice. It's better than fiction because it actually happened. And it's proof that, in the end, love really does conquer all."

Dr. Frank I. Luntz, political and
communications commentator

"Like so many other filmgoers, I was moved, angered, and inspired by the extraordinary documentary *Time*. My only complaint was that it left me wanting to know more. Now, this book goes into greater depth and detail in telling Fox and Rob Richardson's courageous battle to achieve justice for themselves and, ultimately, for so many who have been failed by the American legal system."

Jeffrey Katzenberg, cofounder, WndrCo
and DreamWorks, SKG

"I love this book. Books about people entangled in the American criminal justice system are typically about an individual's personal experience. *Time*, however, is about the journey of a family separated by time, distance, and gun towers of the Louisiana penal system. It's about their decades-long struggle to survive and create a future in the face of none while holding their family together despite a merciless system. For most incarcerated parents, it's an impossible dream. For Fox and Rob Richardson, it's about determination, growth, love, and faith—an inspiring success story against all odds. For me, *Time* is a celebration of the human spirit's ability to transcend the mud and rise from it, unstained like the lotus, bringing beauty into the world where we least expect it."

Wilbert Rideau, award-winning prison journalist, editor
and filmmaker; author of *In the Place of Justice*

TIME

TIME

The **UNTOLD STORY** of the Love

That Held Us Together

When Incarceration Kept Us Apart

FOX AND ROB RICHARDSON

BakerBooks

a division of Baker Publishing Group
Grand Rapids, Michigan

© 2023 by Sibil Fox Richardson and Robert G. Richardson

Published by Baker Books
a division of Baker Publishing Group
Grand Rapids, MI
www.bakerbooks.com

Printed in the United States of America

Library of Congress Cataloging-in-Publication Data
Names: Richardson, Fox (Sibil Fox), author. | Richardson, Rob (Robert G.), author.
Title: Time : the untold story of the love that held us together when incarceration
  kept us apart / Fox and Rob Richardson.
Description: Grand Rapids, MI : Baker Books, a division of Baker Publishing
  Group, [2023] | Includes bibliographical references.
Identifiers: LCCN 2022023117 | ISBN 9781540902641 (cloth) | ISBN 9781493439607
  (ebook)
Subjects: LCSH: Richardson, Fox (Sibil Fox) | Richardson, Rob (Robert G.) |
  Prisoners—Family relationships—Louisiana—Biography. | Prisoners' Spouses—
  Louisiana—Biography. | Prisoners' families—Louisiana—Biography.
Classification: LCC HV8886.U5 R53 2023 | DDC 365/.40922—dc23/eng/20220711
LC record available at https://lccn.loc.gov/2022023117

The authors are represented by the literary agency of Creative Artists Agency, www.caa.com.

Baker Publishing Group publications use paper produced from sustainable forestry practices and post-consumer waste whenever possible.

23 24 25 26 27 28 29   7 6 5 4 3 2 1

To the 2.3 million incarcerated families
still languishing in America's prisons

CONTENTS

FOREWORD

In the face of human suffering, the common impulse is to look away. It is difficult to behold the pain of others. And yet, we are loved by a God who never looks away. There is not a moment in our lives —not the worst or the best moment, the occasion of blissful joy or unbearable suffering—that goes unseen by God. This is the very nature of love: to bear witness.

I have experienced the common impulse to look away throughout my life, but compelled by a God who is our witness, I have endeavored to keep my eyes open and see the beauty, rage, helplessness, redemption, joy, and suffering of those God has put in my path.

As a nun and an activist for the abolition of the death penalty, I have seen suffering. I have seen it in the eyes of the six men I accompanied to their execution in the state of Louisiana during their final moments. I have seen it in the grief of their loved ones as well as the loved ones of the victims of their crimes. I have seen it every time I walk through the iron gates of Angola—the largest maximum security prison in the US.

But I will tell you this: when you look another person in the eye, in the fullness of their human dignity, it is always a sacred moment.

Reading Fox and Rob's profound journey in these pages is just such a sacred moment. This book bears witness to two truths. First, it testifies to the depth to which human dignity can be so desecrated, as those who are incarcerated and their families experience. As Rob writes, life in prison can be like a living death as those made in God's very image are subjected to conditions that make no acknowledgment of this incontrovertible truth. Second, it testifies to the power of hope and love in a way that cannot be denied.

Rarely have I been so moved to witness such a story. *Time* tells the story of two strong-willed individuals determined to live freely and love deeply. Witnessing the ways God has worked in and through them is nothing short of transformative.

Their faith will stir your courage, their love will expand your soul, and their tireless fight for justice will embolden you to speak on behalf of human dignity wherever you find it being dishonored.

Reading this book is an act of witness, of pure presence—may you never forget the transformation of love that you will see in these pages, as I will not forget.

Sister Helen Prejean

INTRODUCTION

ROB

G et your hands in the air and shut up!"
I'd already pulled out my gun. The teller, fear filling her eyes, ran back to the other side of the counter. She'd been trying to reach the door of the vault where another coworker had locked herself in. Now she was anxiously running back and forth as I stood on top of the counter, pointing the firearm. I never intended on shooting it. I just wanted her attention long enough to get the money and leave.

Crack!

The lip of the counter had broken under my weight, and I suddenly went crashing. On my way down to the floor, I sliced my leg along its jagged edges. The teller was frozen. I could hear my nephew Ontario yelling at another teller. He'd already yanked a phone out of the wall after she'd tried to use it to call the police when we first entered the building with our masks on. I would learn a few minutes later, after

13

nearly choking myself, that he'd just sprayed the woman's office with mace.

"Give me the keys to the drawer!" I yelled, gasping for air.

The frozen woman in front of me thawed long enough to throw me the keys and put her hands back up in the air. Desperation started to settle in as I wildly pulled money out of the drawers and dumped it into the blue duffel bag I'd brought with me. That same emotion I felt only moments before we entered the bank washed over me.

Then, I'd been crouched low in the wooded area that was about two hundred yards from the bank. The trees hid the back road where Fox had dropped us off. Between the heat, the mask, and maybe even my own conscience, I felt like I was being strangled. I wore black shorts, which meant that walking through the woods caused me to thrash against thorns and thickets. Fox was perched on top of a hill nearby with binoculars so she could see the front of the bank. As I stood there, being eaten alive by the murderous mosquitos that reigned over Louisiana summers, I couldn't escape this singular thought: *I hate that we have to do this.*

We really did believe there was no other option for us.

"Shots fired, shots fired, officer needs assistance . . ."

FOX

I suppose we *could have* started our story at the end. The awarding of clemency after twenty-plus years of tirelessly petitioning the State of Louisiana to see how the extreme sentencing of Robert was further positioning the state as a leader in the mass incarceration of Black men and women in this country. The heart-wrenching documentary, *Time,* airing on Amazon with stellar reviews. The Oscar nomination. You know, the shinier parts of our story. But as transformative as these last couple of years have been, as grateful as we are for all that has transpired since Rob's release, the end doesn't do much justice to this true narrative. It's really the beginning that offers a much more compelling story.

And in the beginning—1987, to be exact—it was only and always about the love. A radical love that rarely made sense to anyone except us. Which has always been fine, because our love and our faith were what sustained us when our lives were being riddled and torn apart. It was this love that gave us the strength to survive through everything that happened next.

Some may call it cutting class, but I like to say that my friend and I were taking a mental health day. However, Wanda and I *needed* to figure out a ride back to school to finish the rest of the day so our absence would not be reported to our parents. Unfortunately, at sixteen, you don't often work out the details of your shenanigans. As a result, she called one of her church members who was home from the navy to give us a ride. Wanda claimed he was sweet on her and wouldn't hesitate to do it, so I said, "Cool. Hook that up."

We waited at my house, and just like she said, we soon heard a knock at the door. When I opened it, Rob and his friend were standing there.

First reaction? I mean, he was fine. *Okay, Wanda! I see you, girl.*

I let them inside and we all hung out together for a bit

before Rob drove us back over to the school. I spent most of the time talking to Rob's friend because, I mean, Rob was Wanda's man.

ROB

I was *not* Wanda's man.

In fact, I was just there to offer a fellow church member and her friend a ride to school. Fortunately for me though, a really amazing human being answered the door. Maybe it's cliché to say my heart skipped a beat, but that's exactly what it felt like. I'd certainly met girls before, but this felt different. I knew she was somebody I wanted to know more about. Someone I was hopeful to engage on a more personal and intimate level. One thing I certainly knew is that I did not want this to start and end with the encounter at her front door. The only problem was, my partner, Rick, who I'd brought with me, was talking her head off, and I was left to keep Wanda busy—despite us *not* having any kind of relationship. In Wanda's mind, we were one thing, and in mine, we were something else—friends.

Nevertheless, I kept my eyes on Fox. I watched her in my peripheral view as she moved about the house. I tried to see if there was a vibe between us, if she might be interested in me. I needed her to know that I was feeling her. But in that moment, I couldn't get any rhythm from her whatsoever.

FOX

That's because, as far as I knew, he was Wanda's boo. Girl code rules were in full effect.

ROB

I was *not* Wanda's man. And I needed to prove that once and for all.

So we dropped them off back at school and waited until the school day was over to reach out and see if they wanted to hang out more. Rick called Fox, but she didn't answer the phone. We went on with our day, but I really couldn't stop thinking about her. Her face, her smile was stuck in my brain. Later that night, I realized that Rick had called her on my landline, and I hadn't used it since then. Thank God for *69 redial. It was my ticket to getting this girl to know just how much she was in love with me.

FOX

"Who is this?" I said.

"This is Rob, Wanda's friend."

Don't you know this man had the audacity to tell me he was interested in *me*.

"Wanda told me you all were seeing each other."

Now it was my turn to thank God for a telephone service.

"Call her on three-way," he said.

So I did. And as awkward as that call was, sure enough, I learned that my friend had stretched the truth big-time.

It was pretty impressive to me that Rob was feeling me enough that he didn't hesitate to expose Wanda's misrepresentation of their relationship. That night, Rob and I stayed on the phone for hours. Talking about our dreams. Sharing our stories. The next day, not only did I skip class but I skipped school—this time to hang out just with him. He was leaving in two days to go to Norfolk, Virginia, for his next duty station. From our conversations, I learned that Rob came from a military family and, in keeping with his family traditions, had joined the navy. Two days after his high school graduation, he deployed for service. I wanted to get to know this man who was being so honest and transparent with me. When he came over, I experienced something I never had before. To this day, it's hard to describe. He touched my hand, and it was magical. It was the most gentle and caring touch I'd ever received from a man who wasn't my father. I felt his care and compassion, and it created a real ease in my soul.

The rest, as they say, is history.

We share these opening days of our lives together because we need you to know that what sparked for us in that moment when two teenagers held hands was something that would grow and ultimately hold us down during our darkest days. Love is where we began, and it is where we return. And while our love has certainly evolved and transformed over our thirty-five-year journey together—sometimes because of the trauma we both brought to the union—it is also clearly the foundation for everything we have encountered, good or bad, along the way. We were each other's first love and the first person to show the other what love could truly feel like. After all, that is how we learn to love—by first loving.

And honestly, maybe that's what systemic oppression and mass incarceration set out to destroy. Not just the physical body but the capacity for Black and Brown folks to have the love and joy and peace we inherently deserve.

The word is, I was conceived in a brothel. This statement alone could serve as a litmus test for what the rest of my childhood must have resembled. My mother has been married five times and birthed four children into the world. None of us were fathered through those unions. My mother had her first child at fifteen and her second at sixteen. Her parents, Lois and Alex Autrey, who believed firmly in education, said the only way she could go back to school and get her high school diploma was if she let the second child go live with her cousin. And so, my mother did just that. Getting her life back on track, she went as far as obtaining her master's degree and teaching public school for almost forty years before retiring.

By age nine, the father who raised me (who I would later learn was not my biological father) would go from being a larger-than-life entrepreneur and pharmaceutical street salesman to falling prey to his own supply. We became one of the hundreds of thousands of Black families in the 80s hit hard by the epidemic of chemically-engineered crack. But, in my mind and heart, he was still my daddy—the only dad I knew. He was, at his core, a family man who loved me like none other. I was Daddy's girl and the apple of his eye. He was the one who raised me even when he didn't have to. I was still committed to our relationship. So, while he never fully escaped the hold of addiction, when I came home from prison, I took care of him until he made his transition.

So, yes, by society's standards, I was raised in a dysfunctional household. Yet, what I've come to understand from my own experience with parenting is no child comes with a manual. We do the best job we can with the resources, knowledge, and information we have. That is why I often found myself marveling at my mother's determination and drive. No matter the pitfalls or mistakes along the way, she never quit. I hold a deep regard for my mother. She was a teacher who didn't make much money but still managed to maintain a family. Everything she did, she did for what she believed to be the good of her family and for the good of the children she reared alone. Nevertheless, I can't deny that life was challenging for me as a young girl trying to find my way. My mother is a fiery woman. The parenting model that most used in the South was "spare the rod, spoil the child." Even though I grew up never seeing a healthy marriage, somewhere deep down inside of me, I knew it was important.

ROB

Like Fox, I had the experience of growing up in a single parent home; at least, that was the case for a portion of my childhood. But the difference was that my single parent home was headed by my father. I am the youngest of nine siblings, and my biological mother passed away when I was five years old. Hence, my dad was single-handedly responsible for my day-to-day care and supervision. Like Fox's mom, my father had been married five times. My mother was his second-to-last marriage before he transitioned. Ironically, all of my dad's other children were raised under my mother's roof. She reared seven of the nine children that my dad brought into the world.

After my mother passed away, I lived with my dad but also spent some time living with my older sisters and their husbands at different points in my youth. This usually meant on a military base somewhere. In fact, a large part of my early life was spent in a military setting. During one stay with my sister, I lived on Randolph Air Force Base in San Antonio, Texas, where my brother-in-law was on duty. Then, I lived in Kansas City, Missouri, with my sister OJ and her husband, who was a staff sergeant in the army. Finally, after my father met the woman who'd ultimately be his last wife, my stepmom, he decided that I should return home. My sister Anne wanted me to go to Spain with her family. George, her husband, had signed up for overseas duty there, and she believed that experiencing a different culture would help me deal with some of the emotional trauma I endured having lost my mother at such a young age. But Dad was not about to let her take his son all the way to Spain. So, I stayed.

Dad met my stepmother when I was ten, and they eloped a year or two afterward. There definitely was a feeling of preferentialism, although I can't say for sure if it was something that lived in my own little mind, something my older brothers and sisters were putting in my head at the time, or if it really was transpiring.

Nevertheless, life for me was really good at that point. I was my dad's last child, and I'd like to think I was a pretty easy child to manage, for the most part. Fox will say I was spoiled, but I'm not sure that's it. Let's just say that the police were never knocking at my parents' door. Nobody was talking about how I got their daughter pregnant. And I certainly would never ditch school.

FOX AND ROB

Every single one of us has a backstory: the particulars of how we grew up shaped us at a young age and informed how we saw ourselves and the world based on our origin stories. This background establishes who we were and what we'd endured prior to meeting each other. It gives a bit of insight into the baggage we were carrying, and how that baggage manifested into the decisions we made, individually and together. From the time we met in 1987, we dated off and on for ten years. Like most relationships that begin when both parties are really young, we had challenges around communicating what we wanted from each other. Mostly because we were both trying to figure that out for ourselves. Robert got into some trouble while in the military, and that sent us spiraling. In fact, it would be the first of many breakups to come.

Over space and time, we hit the reset button quite often, but the love always brought us back together. So much transpired between our first encounter and the dreadful day both of us ended up in jail for armed robbery. We will share much of that with you in these pages. But, in the way of introduction, we think it is important that you know that our foundation has always been rooted in radical love and unwavering faith. Right or wrong, it was that love that drove us to try and save our business and our family's well-being by any means necessary. It was love that kept us petitioning the courts for twenty years while rearing our six sons. It was love that sparked like kinetic energy in the back of the limousine September 20, 2018, when we embraced for the first time in twenty-one years outside prison walls. And, my God, it was *nothing but* our faith that allowed us to endure it all.

We recognize there are readers thinking, *Well, you committed a crime, so of course you were supposed to do the time.* We get that. We even can accept it. But we also are very clear that sixty years for a first-time felony offense that did not end in death was an egregious sentence born from a system that devalues the humanity of Black men and Black families. We also know that Chase Legleitner, a white man in Florida, committed armed robbery at nineteen and received two years in the county jail.[1] We know that a Black man in the same town, Lamar Lloyd, was sentenced to twenty-six years in prison for the same armed robbery charge.[2] But don't just take our word for it. The United States Sentencing Commission even conducted a four-year-long study, and the key findings were that "Black male offenders continued to receive longer sentences than similarly situated White male offenders."[3]

The bottom line is this: the purveyors of systemic oppression do not see us as inherently valuable. As humans who sometimes make poor decisions. As people worthy of grace or restoration. *That* is as much of a problem as anything.

This isn't an easy story for us to tell. In fact, it would be too easy to dismiss our journey as simply two kids who fell in love, grew up fast, got in trouble, and after a winding road filled with every obstacle one can imagine, found their way back to love. While true in summary, that telling of it feels awfully sophomoric and way too neat. Our story feels more like the place where we grew up. It's the sun on the Louisiana landscape, thick with heat and heavy with longing. It's glorious like the cypress trees that grow out of the murky density of the swamp. It's the way the Spanish moss clings to those trees, holding on to its source, even as it grows.

Likewise, our story is about surviving the heat by holding on to love and faith.

We know firsthand that the economic, emotional, and spiritual impact on incarcerated families is significant, and

that there are millions of families out there who are enduring what we endured. And while we will continue to actively
advocate for those families, we are also aware of the need
for penance. The early Christian church practiced penance
for transgressions as part of the process of reconciliation.
The show of contrition or sorrow for wrongs committed
was a pivotal part of the steps necessary to restore one to
the community.

Having reached a certain level of social awareness, we each
have longed to apologize publicly for the offenses carried out
at our hands more than two decades ago. That said, before
we go any further into sharing our exploits, we would be
remiss if we did not use this as an opportunity to apologize
to the larger body of victims who have suffered as a result of
senseless acts like our own. To the tertiary victims of crime
across our country, we apologize on behalf of ourselves and
the 2.3 million other incarcerated men and women for the
harm we wrought on each of you. We pray that all of you
have found the inner peace you so deserve. Never did we
take into consideration the hurt our actions would cause.
We focused on our own challenges—God knows there were
many—and did not consider the other lives that would be
greatly impacted as a result of our actions. Twenty-plus years
later, we now understand the importance of *all* citizens feeling safe and secure, especially in the places they work and
call home.

We also understand in great detail the importance of not
measuring a person by the worst thing they have ever done.
We are more than the worst thing we have ever done. As much
as accountability is necessary, so is grace.

Our story is about the power of love. How that love continues to adequately sustain us every day. At the end of the day, it's the power of love that enables us to overcome a practical life sentence. It's the power of love that sustained our children when statistics said they were seven times more likely to land in prison. It's the power of love that allowed a single mother to raise six sons in the absence of their father. It was the power of love that allowed us to face the biggest contest of our lives and be victorious. Love forced an unjust system to return to justice. Love gave us the strength to endure the test of *time*. Boy, you talk about a walk of faith!

It is our greatest hope that as you walk in our shoes, you, too, will come to understand and embrace the power of love and what it has the capacity to do when it is employed in the lives of you and yours. As the Bible says best, "God is love. Whoever lives in love lives in God, and God in them" (1 John 4:16).

In Love,
Fox and Rob
April 24, 2022

1

IT FEELS GOOD

Love is our hope and our salvation.
bell hooks, *Salvation: Black
People and Love*

FOX

We had spent over ten years in an on-again, off-again relationship. We had a child together—Remington. Rob had a child, our oldest, Mahlik, from a previous relationship during his lengthy tenure in New Jersey. I had a son, Lawrence, by a man I'd dated during one of our off-seasons. We'd long ago accepted the fact that we would always be connected in some way or another, but whether we'd always be *together*, well, that often depended on the month or the year. By 1997, however, we came to a critical point in our love affair. We were finally willing, if not

27

ready, to commit our lives to one another. But in true Fox and Rob fashion, we would *not* take the easy route.

Finally, things were looking up for me. I'd finished my master's degree at Grambling and had left the abusive relationship I was in with Lawrence's father. I had two children, two degrees, and a newfound hope for my future. I knew that my next step would have to be moving back to Shreveport. With two small children, I understood the value in the "village" and wanted to ensure my sons and I had the support we would all need to be successful. And as God would have it, Rob's time of living in New Jersey had simultaneously come to an end, and he, too, had returned to Shreveport. Back at home, my intentions were set on building my career. I was hoping to either get involved in public service or open my own business—while equally trying to salvage my reputation. Having two kids by two different men and being unwed brought and still brings on undue public scrutiny. People tended to see me as damaged goods no matter my story. So, I focused on my professional development, determined to make something of myself and of my life. I started teaching as an adjunct professor at Southern University while pursuing my doctorate in education. Although I lacked clarity on what I would do with that doctorate, one thing I did know for sure was that I could never go wrong with higher education.

Strangely enough, as I was getting my new life together, Rob was doing the same. He was working full-time and enrolled in cosmetology school with dreams of opening his own barbershop. And as fate would have it, just as my relationship with Lawrence's father had come to a close, so too had Rob's relationship with the young lady he was dating.

When Rob told me that he was looking to get a place, I made the offhand suggestion that, since I had a three-bedroom apartment with just me and the boys, he should move in. In my mind, I was honestly thinking about the convenience of it all. For months, I had been driving back and forth to Grambling twice a week for classes and needed the help.

So I offered, and after wrapping up some unfinished business, he moved in.

It was only supposed to be a roommate/co-parenting situation. But I must admit, the new arrangement had its additional benefits that I enjoyed. Our chemistry had gone absolutely nowhere. But I would not allow myself to envision anything else happening. We were helping each other. Showing up for each other and our children, which was something we'd always done well.

Then I started paying attention. This man was on point about everything. He cooked and cleaned (neither of which are my ministry). He did laundry. I'd come home late at night from teaching, exhausted, and there'd be food on the table, folded sheets and clothes, and the boys were bathed and in bed. Even Lawrence, who was my most demanding child, responded so well to Rob's caretaking, despite him not being his biological father. They'd watch TV together, and my cry-all-day-and-night baby would be so calm in Rob's presence. *I could get used to this*, I thought.

It was heavenly.

I didn't know it would turn into anything more until, one evening, we decided to go together to a friend's birthday party at a pool hall in downtown Shreveport. I'd planned to go with friends, and Rob ended up joining me.

After the party, Rob suggested we take a walk. We strolled along the streets until we came to the Texas Street bridge, a massive steel structure that stretched across the Red River. There were these beautiful lights that gave the path and the bridge itself a gorgeous, romantic glow. The wind was blowing gently, and, on that magical spring night, I fell back into Rob's arms and in love again. I had always loved him, but this time, it wasn't a matter of convenience. He wasn't just my friend or co-parent. He wasn't even just my lover. He was much more. That night, I felt close to him again. Clearly, something bigger was at work.

When we returned home, the fire that was lit at the bridge hadn't died down. The connection was still there. We laid on the couch together and kissed like teenagers again. It was everything. But it also startled me. This wasn't the plan. I pulled out of his embrace.

"Okay, what are we doing here? Are we dating again or what?"

ROB

"I don't want to date you anymore. Ten years is long enough," I said.

I knew that marriage was not necessarily something that she was thinking about. And quite truthfully, it was certainly not something I was thinking about. At least, not consciously. After living together for nearly a month, our lives blended in such a harmonious way that it gave me a clearer vision of what I always knew could be. I'd known Fox for a decade. We had a child together. I knew her mind, body, and soul like it was my own. I didn't want to go on any other fact-finding missions with some other woman I didn't know, trying to figure out if she was the one. I wanted Fox. Yes, because I loved her, but also because things had always been easy with us. Not easy *for* us. Not at all. But our connection never failed. It never faltered.

"So what?! Are you asking me to marry you?" Fox said.

She's always been good at giving language to what I'm feeling. That evening was no exception.

"Yes, I think that's what it would amount to. I'm asking you to marry me."

"When?"

See? She doesn't miss a beat.

"I'd marry you tonight if I could."

"Well, no, I'm not available tonight," Fox shot back.

I couldn't believe this woman. We were talking about marriage, and here she was, making light of my proposal, acting like she was busy or had another hot date later. Like there was anything else she should have been thinking about other than getting married to me. I couldn't help but laugh. I knew exactly who I was getting, and I was cool with all that this entailed.

The truth is, I never fell out of love with Fox. In fact, I have loved her since that day I showed up at her mother's door. As a young man trying to find my way in the world, I admit that I wasn't always the best partner. Nor the most faithful. My promiscuous behavior cost me my relationship with Fox on more than one occasion. So many of our breakups in the past were due to my infidelity. Despite my shortcomings, I realized there was no other woman I wanted to spend my life with. No other person I wanted to build a family with.

I was probably in a similar state of mind as Fox when the subject of marriage came up that night. I was in cosmetology school, working full-time, and had plans of opening a business. I knew the first step in wealth building begins with property ownership. Coupled with the fact that I absolutely enjoyed Fox's company, our chemistry was always off the charts. She was not only the mother of our child but she cared for my child by another woman. She, like me, made no distinction between hers and mine; they were all *our* children. Her heart was huge, and I just wanted to take up permanent residence there, if I hadn't already.

FOX

There was no denying it. He had.

Rob was always home to me. I loved him from day one. But at that point in time, I had zero expectations for him or us. He was just supposed to help with rent and my babies. My heart had been broken one too many times. Yet, the only way I can describe that evening on the bridge and his proposal later that night is that they just felt good. It all felt right. I was moved by his honesty, his vulnerability. By that unseen thing that sets us ablaze whenever he's near me. I felt at ease and, I suppose, safe.

"Well, I'm busy tonight. What about tomorrow?"

Listen, the last time Robert asked me to marry him, I was seventeen years old, and he was trying to get me to move to Scotland with him and finish school there after he'd learned about some of the problems I was having at home. I was moved by his offer, but things for me were a little more complicated than that. I thought he was crazy to even suggest it. And in ten years, he'd never said anything else about that level of commitment between us. So, of course, I had to mess with him a little bit. But the truth is, I knew deep down that Rob had to be serious. He didn't play around when it came to the institution of marriage. It had never been something he had joked about, so I knew, when those words finally came out of his mouth, it meant something.

Where we're from, when someone gets engaged, they usually wait a year or so to plan the wedding. Our engagement quickly got the wheels turning for me. I kept thinking about what type of party I wanted to have. Colors. Table settings. Bridesmaids. But Robert checked all that. He had something else in mind.

"My brother and sister-in-law Ellis and Diane eloped," Rob said.

"Eloped?!" I quipped. I hadn't even thought about that. Rob was concerned because we didn't really have much money, and we both wanted to buy a home for our family. That was extremely important to us. It made better sense to use a little bit of money to elope and save the rest, as opposed to spending our limited resources on a lavish ceremony and reception. So I guess that was it—we were eloping!

That previous summer, I'd taken a trip with the boys to Florida, and we had such a good time. I knew I wouldn't mind visiting again—only this time with the love of my life. My suggestion to Rob was that we should drive to Orlando and get married, and he agreed. We set a date—April 24—and the next day, I was looking up wedding chapels on the computer.

We booked this tiny wedding chapel in Kissimmee, Florida, just outside of Disney World, and within thirty days, we'd sent the kids to their aunt and uncle's house and loaded up our Honda Civic to begin our adventure.

ROB

There was zero apprehension from either of us about what we were doing. It felt like we were kids, bursting with excitement about a family trip to Six Flags or something. And in hindsight, that's exactly who we were. We were kids, eyes glimmering with hope, looking forward to this moment that we'd been secretly longing for all our lives.

FOX

It really was a road trip to remember too. At one point, we had to pull over onto this dirt road because we found ourselves staring down a tornado. The twirling dark mass was right in front of us on the highway, and we had no idea what to do. Everyone we called said, "Take shelter!" But shelter where? There was nothing but fields on either side of us. I was terrified because we were smack-dab in the middle of nowhere with a tornado barreling toward us. I also couldn't help but think it was a sign.

ROB

A sign of what? What she's not saying is that we were probably the cause of that tornado, considering how many pit stops we made to—you know—get a little closer to each other.

FOX

Fortunately, we were able to drive fast enough to get away from the tornado. We weren't going to let anything stop us from getting to Florida and making our love official. Not even a tornado. I'd called a girlfriend of mine who was an event planner and my colleague at Southern, and she'd already helped me brainstorm the logistics.

"I'm going to get married!"

"You're what?" she said.

She couldn't believe it, and if I'm being honest, she wasn't the only one. I was still trying to wrap my mind around this dream come true. Nevertheless, she helped me so much. I didn't think I needed flowers since we were eloping, but she insisted on me having this beautiful bouquet she had made so I'd have something to hold. And I have to admit, they made my wedding pics look so professional. We bought our wedding rings for about $150 each on the last bit of credit I had at the jewelry store. And my Aunt Mattie lent me this classy, white linen dress and gorgeous pearl necklace. I was ready to go. Well, almost. I still needed to get my hair done. Thankfully, when we arrived, Rob noticed there was a hair salon downstairs in our hotel's building and suggested that I go there and get my hair done for our big day!

First thing the following morning, I went to the hotel salon and was shocked to discover that all the stylists there were Asian.

"I'd like to get my hair done," I said squeamishly, very unsure of what they'd say.

"What? What did you say?" a tiny, Asian woman responded.

That's when I told her I was getting married that day and needed to do something with my hair. The woman went into overdrive. I was nervous, as I had never had my hair done by someone outside of my culture. I was worried about whether she could even do Black hair, but she put my fears to rest as she smiled warmly and promised to make me beautiful for

35

my special day. She rushed Rob off to the store to buy some flowers and baby's breath. When it was all said and done, the stylist had given me a beautiful updo with the flowers Rob had retrieved from the store expertly weaved throughout. By the time I left the salon, I felt like such a beautiful bride. And so ready to become Mrs. Richardson—finally!

None of what transpired as it relates to us getting married was planned—at least not in the traditional way. And yet, it somehow *was*. Someone bigger and greater than us was orchestrating it all. I walked down the aisle to Erykah Badu's "Certainly." The lyrics of the song were probably the most befitting to what I was feeling at the time. Especially considering that I had a road home planned and "I was not looking for no love affair." Yet, here I stood, at the altar, ready to take Rob's hand in marriage. Wow! "Who gave you permission to rearrange me? Certainly not me."

Everything just seemed to fall into place. The redheaded woman who married us, a justice of the peace, was so kind and thoughtful. The chapel was warm, quaint, and oh, so beautiful, surrounded by rose gardens on the outside and illuminated by candelabras on the inside. It was enchanting. I said, "I do!" We then whisked off into the night. Our hotel stay included tickets to SeaWorld, so our honeymoon was built into that cost. It was all working out in our favor.

ROB

We decided to spend the evening of our wedding at Disney's Pleasure Island. It was a strip of restaurants, bars, and nighttime entertainment that is now called the Landing and has been absorbed into Disney Springs, a much more family-oriented destination. Back then, though, it was where everyone, tourists and locals alike, would party. Fox and I were on a love high, for sure, so when I saw a DJ, I made a beeline right toward him.

"Hey, can you play a song for me and my girl? We just got married."

When the beat dropped during the intro for Tony! Toni! Toné!'s hit record "It Feels Good," Fox and I looked at each other knowingly. Despite the fact there was no stage, we climbed several feet in the air onto the lip of the massive video projector platform hovering above the people below and began to dance feverishly. It didn't matter that we were the only Black faces in that space. It didn't even matter that maybe they didn't have folks dancing on that platform for safety reasons. We were having a ball. And *nothing* could stop us. We were all the way up!

I'll never forget climbing down and having this large group of partiers applauding us wildly. We felt like rock stars! Our joy was contagious as everyone smiled and *whooped* at us. You would have thought we were on *The Arsenio Hall Show*! We were having the time of our lives.

FOX

But that wasn't even the biggest adrenaline rush of that night. We still needed to consummate the marriage. But, of course, we didn't do it the old-fashioned way. I mean, we did, but that was nothing new for us. We decided to consummate our marriage in a way that, looking back, was so symbolic of the way we lived.

We bungee jumped!

There was a huge skydiving attraction just outside our

hotel. And, up until this particular moment, we hadn't thought much of it. But after returning from Pleasure Island, we both looked at each other and, in an instant, knew that we were going to do it.

Side by side, they strapped us into this steel contraption and raised us three hundred terrifying feet above ground on the world's tallest sky coaster. It felt like God himself was pulling us into the heavens slowly, like the arrow on a bow, preparing to unleash us onto the world. Then they released us into the skies. Terror and joy collided as we soared. We shouted at the top of our lungs. A shout that declared we would not be minimized, we would not be underestimated, and we would not be denied.

That moment was a critical one for both of us. Our shout was a pushback, a prophecy of sorts—we were shouting our countermove against all of the people who'd doubted us. All the systems that held us back. The poor marital role models that we vowed not to replicate. The haters who thought we'd never find our way back to each other. And we were also shouting directly at ourselves. The poor choices we'd made. The mistakes. It was a way for us to declare that our trajectory was changing. It was a way for us to give our hopes and dreams air. Our passions were finally aligned, and our children were going to have it so much better than we did.

On the way home, we planned our lives. We were going to buy a house (we'd just gotten word that a closing date had been set) and open a business. We believed with our whole hearts that we could conquer it all. The sky was the limit for us. With God and each other, we were invincible.

Tony! Toni! Toné! was right—life really did *feel good*.

2

FOR THE CULTURE

When a man is denied the right to live the life he believes in, he has no choice but to become an outlaw.

Nelson Mandela, *Long Walk to Freedom*

FOX AND ROB

We had ambition. We had courage. We had the *desire* to have better and be better. But the challenge was, we did not always have the support. We didn't have the mentorship or the best business guidance. That's why in one moment we were growing our family and starting a business—Shreveport's first hip-hop clothing store, Culture—and in the next moment, we were desperately trying to save it all by doing the worst thing we could have done. We were at once hoping for a life we'd never seen and also walking into a living hell as we watched our dreams fall apart.

As soon as we returned from our wedding and honeymoon, we signed for what would be our family's first home. It was the perfect starter home. With three bedrooms, two bathrooms, an open floor plan, a one-car garage, and a back deck that was to die for, it was the ideal home for all the family gatherings and cookouts we planned to host.

We then turned our attention toward securing a space for our business. The first step was what we called "field tripping." In the spring and summer of 1997, we traveled across the country on field trips to visit other successful hip-hop clothing stores like Dr. Jay's in New York and Alexander's Hip Hop Shop in Atlantic City. Our goal was to learn as much as we could about running this type of business, what to look for, and possible pitfalls. There is no greater adventure in life than being in the pursuit of one's dreams.

One of the most valuable pieces of advice we received during that time was from Tito, the store owner in Atlantic City, who we considered a mentor. We were fixated on all the niceties and other nonessentials when Tito abruptly turned to us and snarled, "Just get open!" He said it was too easy to start overthinking what we needed when our primary objective should be *to just get the doors opened*. The truth was, small Black-owned businesses like ours would not likely see the capital necessary to really fund our ventures properly. And we certainly didn't have the ability to lay away six months of our salary as a cushion. So it was all about taking the leap and building momentum after launching. That became our plan. We would put a month or two of rent down on the place and maybe raise enough to get the first round of inventory and whatever small things we needed.

On another one of our trips, we headed farther south, where we met with the owner of For the Soul in You, the first and only hip-hop clothing store in Houston. She was adamant about us attending the world's largest trade show for clothing retailers, MAGIC in Las Vegas. This was where urban brands like FUBU and Maurice Malone first got their recognition. She'd said nothing but a word! We didn't think twice about heading to Vegas. If the MAGIC show was where we needed to be, that's where we were going to be.

ROB

We weren't looking to duplicate what other stores were doing. Hip-hop is about originality. We wanted to learn more about what worked and what didn't. In business terms, I guess we were trying to find the best practices of those who were doing what we wanted to do. But the one thing I was adamant about was not trying to emulate what people were doing on the East Coast. We always intended to make sure that our Louisiana culture and swag were obvious and could be felt in our store. That said, we couldn't deny that these stores knew what they were doing in their markets, so we tapped them for information. When the owner of For the Soul in You said go to MAGIC, that was it! We set our sights on trying to get registered and doing what we needed to do in order to get proper licensing and other things in preparation for our launch.

FOX

We were on it! In May of that year, we found a building that we thought was going to be the perfect spot for Culture. There was an older gentleman we knew who was trying to get out from under some property he owned on Greenwood Road, a main thoroughfare on Shreveport's west side. The space was formerly a carpet warehouse, and it felt like it was perfect for everything we wanted to do. Our goals weren't just about elevating our family. We wanted to do something for our community. In addition to the clothing store, we envisioned a community bookstore that sold African and African American art. An event center. A barbershop and beauty salon. The space was definitely large enough to make all of these businesses come to fruition. In our minds, it would be like the Haus of Fox and Rob.

ROB

We were committed to making this work. After all, what was going to stop us? We were both working and had supplemental incomes. That spring, I was in barber school and I had the first disbursement of my student loan money. In addition, I was waiting on an insurance settlement from a car accident, all while running my mobile detail business. In my mind, I was ballin'! Fox was teaching in the city at Southern University while working on her doctorate at Grambling State. She was also selling Mary Kay on the side. It wasn't much, but we had no reason to believe that we didn't have what we needed to make things work. To our surprise though, Southern decided to drop its Public Administration program.

Hence, Fox was notified that her teaching position would come to a close at the end of the summer.

FOX

That's when we were hit with our first significant financial setback. We didn't realize all the trouble we'd run into with the house we'd just purchased. After we bought it, we found out the foundation was cracked and the roof was bad. We'd purchased the house through the Housing and Urban Development program (HUD). Unbeknownst to us, the house had some serious problems, including costly structural damage. Our dream was turning into a nightmare right before our eyes. We made some adjustments along the way and started looking at other ways to market our new business venture and generate capital. This led to a direct marketing campaign, scouring neighborhoods with flyers, and going door-to-door selling memberships to our future customer base. We got the idea from the best—Sam Walton, the founder of Walmart. Back in the early- to mid-80s, he had a street team that went door-to-door offering Sam's Club memberships in our neighborhoods. Needless to say, it worked for Sam, but it didn't work for us.

ROB

I mean, to be fair, it was our first home purchase. We didn't know what to look out for. Like most young people in their twenties, we thought we knew everything and had it all figured out. We were venturing to do something that no one else in our family or social circle had ever done before. Opening a retail clothing store in 1997 featuring clothing by Black designers was not only a new concept but it was unheard of in our region of the country. It was far outside of the wheelhouse of anyone we knew. Folks around us were far less traveled and couldn't see our vision nor understand our dream, a truth that we found to be difficult for others to grasp. Making our dream of Culture a hard sell.

We soon realized that not only had we purchased a lemon for a home but the site of Culture was not in an ideal location for retail sales. While the building where Culture would be housed was big enough for us to build out and do everything we wanted, it was also in a more industrial area of the city. In fact, we learned that the entire street was considered an industrial district. You should have seen the way we'd flag down cars, trying to get people to pull into our spot. There was plenty of traffic but none that stopped. Fox and I had violated the three most fundamental principles of business: location, location, location.

FOX

So three months into our marriage, we had a house with a leaking roof and cracked foundation, the lost income of my teaching position, and a business that was in the wrong location. And the hits just kept coming. Our son, Lawrence, who was one year old at the time, had to be rushed to the emergency room and then hospitalized for some undiagnosed ailments that left us with a ton of unexpected medical bills. By the time we got to July, our hearts were broken, and we were spinning out of control trying to figure out how to make everything work.

MAGIC was the first week in August, and we held on to hope that if we could just get there, we could climb our way out of the widening hole that threatened to swallow us and our dreams. At that same time, I had recently reconnected with a mentor through my involvement with the Shreveport Chamber of Commerce and the Black Business Association. He told me that whenever I got ready to open a business he'd be willing to help me. I told him about Culture and explained that we needed a $50,000 cash injection in order to get the first round of inventory in place. He seemed excited about the opportunity and even told me he consulted with his accountant. Unfortunately, I didn't get any of that enthusiasm or an agreement in writing.

This, too, would later come back to bite us.

Hope is a heavy thing, and we were carrying it with all the strength we had. We were in hot pursuit of the American dream, and the energy of our naysayers only fueled our determination. We were moving in the spirit of those who believe that the impossible translates into "I'M POSSIBLE." The rhetoric of the American dream imposes an unrelenting optimism without consideration of the systemic factors that aren't equally distributed. Nevertheless, it can be a motivating force that propels people to achieve and accomplish things that they might not otherwise strive for. It was definitely that way for us. Our dream's elusiveness made it that much more compelling for us. When one's dream always seems to be out of reach, it feels like it's very much worth the pursuit. So Vegas, we were coming for you.

ROB

We were out of there! We borrowed Fox's mother's car, a Delta 88, and drove more than 1,050 miles across the country and through the desert to make our dreams come true in Las Vegas. Another couple who were friends of ours tagged along with us because they were interested in opening a shoe store. For us, it was as if we were on our way to the land of Oz to see the mighty wizard and were taking others who dared to dream along with us. We drove more than twenty hours, with the pedal to the metal in Ms. Peggy's Oldsmobile, only stopping occasionally to take in the alluring sights.

When we arrived, MAGIC was, well, *magical*. We met so many key figures in urban wear. We ordered clothes and took pictures with the founders of FUBU and countless others, including the legendary hip-hop group Naughty by Nature, whose brand was everywhere and on everything at the time. It was a star-studded weekend with all the events and private parties. One such party was at a nightclub called the Drink. The line was stretched across the parking lot. Fox and I realized we had to come up with a plan if we wanted to get in, seeing as how we were not on the list. But to our surprise, one of the sales reps we'd met earlier walked up. Fox stopped him and explained our dilemma.

"Say less," he said, and we followed him into the VIP entrance as part of his entourage.

Once inside, we looked at each other and said, "Love it when a plan comes together." We had secured entrance into one of the most exclusive parties of the weekend. The venue was electric with all the flashing lights and music that vibrated every surface. It was packed wall-to-wall with industry moguls gathered in roped-off sections. That night, we hobnobbed with executives and fashion aficionados, and we watched some of the most dynamic performances by hip-hop artists.

———

We still had house problems, and our store was still in a challenging location, but that magical night, things seemed like they were looking up. It didn't matter what had failed before or what was falling apart in the present. We were clear that the future was bright, and all would be well. We put a little elbow grease to our faith and the sky was the limit as far as we were concerned. With $50,000 coming in from Fox's investor, we were returning to Shreveport poised to build something amazing for our family and our city.

There was only one more problem. When we got back to Louisiana, we went to meet with our investor—*together* this time. We thought we were going to pick up a check. What we actually got was a slap in the face. And that was something we totally didn't expect.

A brown-skinned man with a low, uniform afro and beady eyes that loomed behind his thick bifocals, a man we thought was our key investor, barely looked up when he spoke from behind his imposing desk.

"I've changed my mind," our investor said. He denied us without explanation.

"What do you mean, 'changed your mind'?" Fox said.

I just sat there, confused and angry.

"How is that even possible? We have clothes on the way," Fox continued.

"Like I said, I changed my mind," he said, effectively ending the conversation.

It felt like he had spat on us. But we were still determined. He wasn't going to stop us if we could help it. I looked this man dead in the eyes and said, "Okay, well they say what doesn't kill you makes you stronger. Thank you for making us stronger."

We walked out of that office seeing stars from all the anxiety and desperation that had started to settle in our souls.

———

It was the dead of summer, and those next few days in August were the darkest either of us had ever known. The heat seemed to magnify the painful place we found ourselves in. We still had hope, but that hope was fading away with each day as the medical bills loomed, the past due mortgage payments piled up for a house that was falling apart, and of course, the shipment of clothes was pending. I'd managed to negotiate a pretty sweet deal with the owner of the warehouse where the store was going to be located, but even that note was coming due. He allowed us to pay rent, $1200, every other month, which meant we could have some breathing room as we built up traffic in the space. The warehouse owner also threw in a newly remodeled two-bedroom home that was just around the corner from the warehouse. No, it didn't occur to us to move into that space when things got tight. Instead, we chose to move our cousin into the house and charge him $400 a month for the rent. In our minds, we figured that by the time our cousin pays two months of rent, that would be two-thirds of what we needed to pay the owner. But the remaining $400 every two months might as well have been a billion dollars in light of the other bills. In our young twentysomething minds, it felt like an insurmountable amount of money.

All of this was weighing heavily on us. We'd sunk to a lowly place as a result of the rejection that caught us so far off guard. We didn't anticipate it. We didn't see it coming. But now that it had happened, we plummeted to a place in our souls that opened a door for all kinds of thoughts to give rise.

FOX

Our financial challenges were toppling us. We were reduced to eating leftover commodities and rummaging coin jars for gas money. Nevertheless, we still needed to be present for each other. For our children. For our families. But how would we do that and still keep this dream alive? How would we do that with very little guidance? We didn't know what we didn't know. I trusted this man. But in hindsight, maybe I missed something. Why wouldn't he put his offer in writing? Had his initial interest in investing been because I was a young, beautiful, vibrant woman? Did he not like Rob? We left without an answer. There were so many feelings such as sorrow, despair, and guilt that we both had to tuck away for the sake of our own sanity.

The thing that hurt the most is the fact that we felt like our dreams were slipping away. We'd gotten bold enough to chase them. We'd actually begun to feel like they were in reach. And yet, they were snatched away from us before we could even get out of the gate. But we were going to figure it out, even if that meant doing something we would later regret. Rob decided to embark on another venture. One that seemingly guaranteed regular cash flow but came with its own set of risks and compromises.

Whatever faith we had waned to an all-time low. Our lives were strictly about survival. We stole gas, food, and cable whenever and however we needed to. So many people talk about a faith walk as something that is pristine and without blemish. That's not what we've experienced. Sometimes a faith walk is one that finds you in the trenches and lifts you out, even when you have dirt all over you. And that is a different walk of faith than the kind we borrow from our mamas and grandmothers. It would be these trials and the ones to come that would teach us how to develop a faith of our own, one that requires us to trust the process even when there doesn't seem to be any light at the end of the tunnel.

ROB

Fox is being delicate, but I will tell it to you straight. I started moving drugs just to get by. I suppose I thought that if I could at least get the money we needed to help us catch up on all our past due bills, then I could step away from that life and pour my heart into building the business. But, until then, I traveled up and down the same roads that wiped out millions in our communities in the 1980s and 90s. I knew it wasn't right, but for me, at the time, it was the wrong that was the most right. God bless my soul.

FOX

While Rob was doing what he felt like he had to do, I tapped all my resources. I tried to get a bank loan. Denied. I talked with people in both our families who we knew had access to capital. Denied. It felt like everybody's response started with "What are you asking for?" and ended with a firm and resolute "Hell no!"

The strangest thing was, we continued to go forward with the launch of the store. Despite not knowing where the money was coming from, we continued promoting the opening of Culture, even being featured in a sprawling article in the Shreveport newspaper's business section announcing that in October 1997, our business was going to be open.

In hindsight, I suppose we could have stopped. Pushed back the launch. Decided to press pause until we could regain control of our finances and lives. But each time I considered doing so, I couldn't help but hear the voices of those who didn't believe in us. We did not want to face what we thought would have been a devastating level of ridicule and public humiliation. We were opening in October. Period.

In many ways, we were operating purely on vision and blind ambition alone. We didn't have the knowledge we needed to execute the dream properly. We also did not have any reputable mentors. Nobody was ministering in our lives. We now know the importance of having a wise person to share our decision with, someone to draw from. But back then, we only had each other. We only had our fear. Fear of what other people would think about us. Fear of failure. Fear of the unknown. And when fear is driving, a crash is inevitable.

The other piece is this: we were stuck thinking about the wrong thing. Addressing the wrong need. We kept thinking that if we just had the money, then everything else would be okay. Thinking it was only about the money, we hyperfocused on it and ultimately ended up trading our whole family for the possibility of it. We had love. I had my husband. My children had their father. And I would lose all those things that mattered the most to me for something of much lesser value.

ROB

I'll never forget that day. Fox and her girlfriend had recently watched the popular movie *Set It Off*, featuring Jada Pinkett Smith, Queen Latifah, Vivica A. Fox, and Kimberly Elise.[1] The movie followed four women who, fed up with a system that seemed to keep them perpetually behind, decided to rob the bank where one of them had been unjustly fired. One day, Fox's friend jokingly said, "We should rob a bank." Fox shrugged it off and said, "Man, are you crazy? I have kids." But I think, when she shared that with me, a tiny seed had been planted. I kept thinking, *Before I let my family fail, I will take the money we need*.

FOX AND ROB

In our young minds, there was no other way around it. No other options, not with the potential of public embarrassment looming and debts piling high. We had kids to feed and a home to salvage, so we were going to do whatever we needed to do. We sat in the car one day and looked at each other with the weight of the world made clear in our eyes. What were we going to do? How were we going to do it?

The unjust systems all around us had already done their tragic and devastating work. They told us that we were not worthy of help. They said, despite having no prior issues, a couple of degrees, and plenty of service, this wasn't enough for a loan or grant. The transgenerational poverty that had permeated parts of our families gave us the incentive of wanting to break the curse, only we were left without the necessary tools to do so. The residue of the transatlantic slave trade that tore families apart and the Jim Crow laws that tried to limit and stifle our growth as citizens meant that our families were already operating at a deficit. The wealth gap is real. The disparities in family dynamics are real. We saw that with our own eyes.

And of course, "all skinfolk ain't kinfolk," as the elders say. The man who broke his promise of investing in our business was a Black man who couldn't see beyond his own misogyny and lust to truly help another Black couple grow. To be clear, naming the systems at work isn't a way for us to escape accountability, as some might think. It's more so a way to name all the factors at play. We never believed that we were owed something simply because we are Black, although there are some arguments out there that would say we were and are for the sheer reason that our ancestors were and are owed payment for the greatest infringement on their humanity. Nevertheless, we've always been the kind of people who'd bust our tails to see our vision come to pass. The work ethic was there. The vision was there. We just wanted what so many others are freely given—help.

When our help didn't come, we became desperate. And

desperate people do desperate things. Believing there were no other options, we half-heartedly decided to rob a bank. It was a botched attempt that ended in a foot chase, gunshots, and subsequent arrests. Rob and Ontario were captured exiting the dense wooded area alongside the bank, where they were cuffed, read their rights, questioned, and later jailed on a $300,000 bond for armed robbery and aggravated battery charges. And just like that, the dreams we had for our lives crumbled to dust.

3

BOND, BABIES,
AND CONVICTION

I am convinced that imprisonment is a way of pretending to solve the problem of crime. . . . It is a cruel and useless substitute for the elimination of those conditions—poverty, unemployment, homelessness, desperation, racism, and greed—which are at the root of most punished crime.

Howard Zinn, *You Can't Be Neutral on a Moving Train*

FOX AND ROB

Faith has a cyclical nature. A recurring theme in Scripture is that God gives us life and gives it abundantly. But then, the human heart is usually tempted in some way, shape, or form. We yield to temptation, and while that isn't the way of God and repentance is necessary, the beautiful thing is that salvation is still possible. God offers us salvation as we move through our recovery, and then—the most glorious thing—our story can start again. With salvation comes rebirth and renewal. Our journey has very much felt like that abundance-temptation-repentance-salvation process. We started off with this beautiful, albeit unorthodox, beginning. We were feeling good and powerful. And then, when trials and tribulations hit, we fell to temptation. We fell to our lack of mentorship and other healthy relationships. We fell to our fear, financial instability, and cultural influences. And all that created the perfect storm. The perfect environment for devastation. Thankfully, salvation was on the horizon. It would just take many years to see it.

After Rob and Ontario's arrest for the armed robbery in September 1997, both were sent to jail to await trial or until they were able to be released on bond. Fox was released on her own recognizance but also awaited arraignment for her part as an accessory to the crime.

FOX

"What in the hell were you thinking?"

I was so broken by everything that when I came home and told my mother that we'd robbed a bank, her words felt like daggers in my heart. I was devastated by what we had done. It was fear of embarrassment that led us to rob the bank, but the embarrassment and humiliation of having made that choice was far worse—the irony!

I was scared of the potential outcomes. If both Rob and

I were in prison, what would that do to our babies at the ages of three and six? It was so hard to even fathom such a thing. So hard to see what should have been clear before we ever took that route.

But I was also very determined. We'd done this horrible thing to save our store. I was not going to let what Rob was going through, what we all were going through, to be in vain. I was going to open Culture against all the odds.

My mother was not happy about this at all. She kept telling me that I needed to "take that sign off the front of the building, put it in storage, and go get yourself a job." I understood what she was trying to say, but I also knew that, because I was facing criminal charges, I was never going to be able to get a nine-to-five. There was no turning back for me. If we had risked it all for this business, I was not going to let us down. To raise money, I started throwing parties and comedy shows in the back of the warehouse. We had some gifted talent come through over the course of that next year.

Getting Culture off the ground while Rob was in jail and I was waiting to go was truly an all-hands-on-deck endeavor. A collection of youths from around the community and I built a homemade stage, and I used the little bit of money I made from the parties I threw to buy store fixtures and get a few of the pieces that we had ordered shipped in. And while it was a month later than we'd hoped, Culture—Shreveport's first original hip-hop clothing store—had a grand unveiling on November 1, 1997. Six weeks after we'd robbed a bank and Rob had gone to prison.

As far as my boys and I, we were struggling something terrible. Our house was still falling apart, but I put a tarp over the broken roof and was still able to find someone to rent it out. Meanwhile, my babies and I were living in the back of the store with no hot water. Every day, I'd boil water on the stove that was in the little kitchenette in the back of the store, and we would all take sponge baths before our day. I'd sit the boys in the sink and bathe them before sending them to school. We had also put bunk beds in the back room of the store. In another room, we put a sleeper sofa that I had from college. We rented the sleeper sofa to a young woman who needed a place to stay, and the boys and I slept on the bunk beds. We all lived there for a year. I was in strict survival mode.

But I did all of that with a small sense of pride. I'd decided that I wasn't going to hold my head down. I was definitely living with a traumatized state of mind, but I'd chosen to go numb in order to simply survive the day. I had no idea what they were going to do to Rob, nor how I could get him home or out on bond. I didn't even know how we were going to simultaneously maintain the business while addressing this beast of a criminal justice system that speaks a whole other language than the one we were familiar with. All we could do was try. Rob and I wrote letters back and forth to each other and spent the majority of our calls and correspondence in the spring of 1998 trying to strategize and plan for the business. During this same time, I won the young, rising business leader of the year award given by the Shreveport Chamber of Commerce.

Culture was the talk of the city that year. As hard as it was behind the scenes, our business was unlike anything anybody had ever seen before. It became common to see my boys or me somewhere in the city passing out flyers about sales or events. Standing on a corner in the middle of the main intersection of a highway, Remington would turn that beautiful face toward passersby, and they'd have to take a flyer from his little hand. I wouldn't be far away, with Lawrence in a carrier on my back sleeping or playing. When people came for the comedy shows, we'd throw an impromptu fashion show during intermission. This small town was thrilled to have something to do that felt very much like the events they'd seen on television. So, while we were facing robbery charges, I was gaining recognition as a local business leader and sending Rob the most fly clothes in jail.

ROB

And I loved it. Even though I was in prison, I didn't feel disconnected from what was going on because Fox made sure I didn't. The one thing that was pretty consistent throughout most of our incarceration journey is that we always found a way to keep the communication lines open. Even if that meant something wasn't going to get paid or something else wasn't going to get the attention it needed, we were going to make sure we called or sent letters. I was rarely out of the loop. Fox and I have always brainstormed together. We have always been in sync with one another, tapping each other for ideas. So much of what Fox was thinking to do next was the result of brainstorming she and I may have done the previous night over the phone or during her visitations.

If anything, I felt a sense of vulnerability by what she was experiencing in my absence. I could help her when it came to generating ideas, but I couldn't protect her. I couldn't protect my boys. A year into Culture's opening, people started breaking into the store. This left me very anxious because, knowing they were living in the back of the store, I was constantly wondering whether they were safe. It's quite the juxtaposition when you consider that my own actions had made others feel unsafe and unprotected.

I realize that so much of what we were doing, trying to do, was reactive. People often ask why didn't we consider all of this in the first place? Play out all the potential outcomes? Those are great questions. It's crazy how, when we find ourselves in a quagmire, all the stuff we should have thought about prior to getting stuck starts rushing to our memories. Sometimes it's too late. Other times, it's just in the nick of time. Fox and I were solely focused on getting open. So that's what Fox did. We dealt with the rest as the rest came along.

I remember us having conversations about the stories we'd read about immigrants who came to this country and, until their businesses got off the ground, they'd often have their entire families living on-site. Communal living was not just a cultural holdover from their home, it was a sacrifice they were making. They weren't afraid to be a little uncomfortable if it meant abundance down the road. And that's how we saw things. We had certainly proved that we were willing to do whatever was necessary to see our dreams come true, so this would be no different.

At least it was until I began to see how Fox's and the boys' lives were in danger.

FOX

Listen, I was on it. I wasn't trying to be there any longer than I had to. So as soon as we could leave, we did. In the meantime, Rob was working on the inside to get money we needed for the business, our family, and our legal woes, and I worked on the outside to do the same. When most people think about incarcerated relationships, they think about some poor woman taking care of some man who sold her a pipe dream. But for us, it's always been a partnership, above and beyond anything else. Rob always found a way to come through and contribute in some significant manner, even if it wasn't always about dollars and cents. Even if it was making a call to someone he knew could help or finding a resource that could help. He never sat idle in prison just waiting to see what I was going to do.

ROB

That's true. I'm always amazed at how, at very crucial points in my incarceration, I would gain favor from not just the other guys but also the administration. And admittedly, I used that favor to my advantage for the benefit of my family and the business. Before being moved to Angola, I was initially jailed at Lincoln Parish Detention Center in Ruston (about an hour outside of the city of Shreveport). Because I came in with cosmetology expertise and they didn't have an on-site barber in the jail, I became the go-to barber inside of the prison. In exchange for the warden allowing me to have my barber tools, I agreed to be the official barber for both the incarcerated and the staff. I also made a little bit of money cutting hair, which would offset the times when money was tight at home and Fox could not send me anything.

As I was cutting the hair of security officers though, I was able to squeeze out other favors. Extra visiting time. Extra phone time. And it was a wrap when Fox sent me clothes from the store. I'd resell them to the officers, who started to look forward to those shipments. It became the talk of the prison. Some of the guys would say, "Rob has a big-time clothing store in Shreveport"; "Did you see the logo on his package? That's his store"; "Rob has something going on outside of here."

As good as it felt knowing Fox was getting awards and being praised for her work in the business, it felt equally good to get recognition inside the prison. It felt rewarding to me, as small of an effort as it was, to be her sounding board and idea man. It felt good for me to be able to get visits. Even when our visits with one another were terminated as the legal proceedings started to take a turn, it made me feel good to be able to send whoever came to visit back home with money from the clothes I had sold. Sure, it wasn't much. But if nothing else, I still had hope that I could be of assistance to the person who was going all out to assist me.

On the legal side of things, we were facing a hard road. We had already endured fourteen months of failed plea attempts facilitated by Paul Kidd Sr., an attorney who neither Fox nor I considered to be effective, to say the least. Less than thirty days after my initial arrest, I had accepted a plea offer of ten to eighteen years at the advice of former counsel Richard "Rick" Gallot II, who Fox had retained to represent us. Following the presentence investigation, a recommendation was made to the judge that I would be a great candidate for IMPACT (an intervention program for first offenders). The hurdle was that I needed a sentence of seven years or less, and

Rick didn't believe he could get the judge to budge. But attorney Kidd believed he could indeed "get me a better deal." He was referred to me by the young white female parole officer who conducted my presentence investigation. After a few talks, we hired him. Kidd's first piece of advice was for us to withdraw our guilty pleas, and in November 1997, Kidd signed on as counsel of record, entered several pretrial motions, and had us withdraw our guilty pleas. Later, we learned that this was a disastrous move, as it reexposed us to the ninety-nine-year maximum sentence for armed robbery. After months of failed plea attempts, we eventually sought a different exit strategy.

Posting bond was now the strategy for release. Kidd enlisted then Monroe, Louisiana, senator Charles Jones, who Kidd believed could be helpful in our bond reduction proceedings. Jones filed a motion to reduce bond. Subsequently, my $300,000 bond was cut in half.

I then reached out to a local bail bondsman who agreed to come see me at the jail. In our briefing, he simplified the bond process. The breakdown was like this: a nonnegotiable 6 percent of the bond goes to the state, 3 percent goes to the bail bondsman who bonds you out, and then 3 percent goes to the power—the company insuring the bond—assuming that the bond is over $100,000. Essentially, he was saying I could negotiate what I owed both the bail bondsman and the insurer. This was amazing news! When it all shook out, we only needed to come up with $9,000 for me to bond out as opposed to the whopping $36,000 we had initially thought.

Navigating the criminal justice system was akin to solving for the order of operations in math.

To solve for x, you have to simplify the problem. In life, the big picture is oftentimes overwhelming and will leave you defeated before you start.

For me, freedom $= x$.

FOX

Interestingly, I happened to be in court and ran into another bail bondsman who gave me the contact number of a guy in Shreveport he believed would bond Rob out. Armed with this information, I had what I needed to negotiate Rob's release. The only problem now? I needed the money.

So, I went back to what had worked in the past. I threw a comedy concert for the ages in the back of our warehouse to raise the money. The place was so packed that there were people who tried to shut the show down, complaining about the noise. But I wasn't having it. I had not only brought these comedians to Shreveport but I had booked them for Grambling and Monroe that same weekend. I went on the radio, KGRM Tiger 91.5, to promote the concert, and I shouted out Rob's name every single time I was on air.

ROB

It was everything. Whenever Fox would shout out to me on the radio, there would be a roar from inside the jail cells. It was insane.

FOX

That concert weekend brought in all the money we needed, so I reached out to my contact at Dement Bailbonds. We'd previously learned through the grapevine that there were some "official people" who had put the word out to not let Rob out. This scared away all of the local bail bondsmen who might have helped. But Dement played by their own rules. And on February 2, 1999, we were going to pull up to the Lincoln Parish Detention Center at 7:00 a.m. and request Rob's release!

ROB

I felt a high level of excitement at the thought that I would be bonded out and returned to my family. I'd been locked up for nearly a year and a half at that point, so to see the light of day, to be on the other side of the cage, was indescribable. Going to breakfast, listening to the morning announcements, and then hearing the guard tell me that I needed to "roll my stuff back"—another way of saying I needed to get ready to go home—had my body buzzing. As is the case with most people facing charges, the men around me were sleeping the time away. But on this morning as they slept, I slipped out of cell G and headed for the front gate. Posting bond was a small victory in an admittedly long and arduous journey toward regaining our freedom.

FOX

Listen, I jumped right in Mama's car and drove the bondsman down to bail out my baby. Honestly, it felt like I was a thief in the night. Yes, I knew that bond, with all its problematic hoop-jumping, was a fundamental right for everyone. But it still felt like we were stealing something.

ROB

Like stealing freedom.

We'd run into so many obstacles. From the system not wanting to correct the books to reflect the actual amount of my bond, to having to hire a lawyer to get the wrongful charges removed, to Paul Kidd withdrawing from our case when he concluded that we were not willing to pay for a trial following his failed plea attempts, to all the extra procedures the bail bondsman was forced to go through when he came to pick me up. There was so much extraordinary suspicion that even the bondsman felt like he was a coconspirator.

FOX

But it didn't matter what they thought, or what foolishness they tried to throw our way. Rob was coming home.

ROB

When I walked out the front gate and saw Fox sitting in the backseat of that car, my heart started beating like African drums. When we pulled off, I still had so much trepidation in my heart. I thought they were going to stop us at the gate or on the road. It wasn't until we got on I-20 and headed toward Shreveport that I could truly breathe.

FOX

I was crouched in the backseat of the car trying not to be seen. Keep in mind, I was facing charges too. I didn't even want them to know I was in town. I thought they'd come out and rearrest me if they knew I was out there. I'd find out later my intuition was right.

Nevertheless, at that moment, we were flying high. No one could tell us nothing.

The bail bondsman laughed at us as we drove into the city. "Alright, now. I know y'all. Don't go having twins," he said.

ROB

And where was our first stop after dropping off the bondsman? 4114 Greenwood Road. The birthplace of Culture, Shreveport's original urban clothing store. We parked, got out of the car, and Fox handed me the keys to the store. I opened the door and entered the place that held a ghostly essence. Fox had relocated Culture just months prior, so we were standing in the empty room that once held so many of our dreams. It was hard to believe that so much had transpired in that space. We'd laughed out loud there. Cried in silence there. Launched campaigns and created refuge and job opportunities for young aspiring teens in our community there. We had experienced some amazing victories and suffered some awful defeats. But above all, we did what we said we were going to do.

FOX

To be able to touch my husband, in the privacy of our own space, after nearly two years, sent my head spinning. It was definitely magical. Not only because we were separated by prison walls but because my visits, in general, had been restricted at the parish jail because of our case. I wasn't allowed to even see him for a year during that time. It was all just letters and phone calls.

ROB

We were together again. Feeling invincible again. Nothing could stop us.

Afterward, we made our way across town to South Park Mall, to the new location. It was a beautiful homecoming. My cousin ET was the store manager, working alongside two other part-time workers. The vibrant colors of urban fashion lines illuminated the 950-square-foot space.

But it didn't take long for the elation to turn to a hard and difficult understanding. Yes, I was home on bond, and yes, we managed to relocate Culture, but we still had to deal with the charges that loomed. We had to figure out how to restore our fumbled plea bargain and how to minimize the sanctions they were looking to hand out to us.

FOX

According to the original plea deal, I would accept probation in exchange for my role in the crime. I had no expectation that I would serve any time in prison. And at that point, I had yet to be arraigned on my charges. But that was also about to change. Later in February, my attorney contacted me and said I needed to be in court the next day. Now that I'd bonded Rob out, they'd suddenly decided to bring me in for arraignment. I was totally caught off guard. Rob, the boys, and I were just starting to feel a sense of normalcy. The day of my unexpected hearing was the same day our company was sponsoring Remington's kindergarten class field trip.

I was so angry that I had to be in court that morning that I sent a fax to the attorney—who I already had reservations about—firing him. When I showed up in court the next day, he told the judge I had fired him, and when it was all said and done, my bond was raised to $100,000, and they re-arrested me.

I paged Rob "911," which was the code we used when there was a potential for things to go bad in court. By the time I got Rob on the phone, they had already started the intake booking process. I was angry and terrified. *It's not supposed to go this way*, I thought. The idea of spending my first night in jail was too much.

That's when Rob pulled off one of the most amazing feats ever witnessed in our thirty-five-year tenure together when he convinced Ms. Peggy, my mom, and two of her most conservative and eldest sisters Pinkie and Coral Jean to put up their homes as collateral for my six-figure bond. After getting the kids settled and tucked away for the evening, Rob and the bondsman hit the road to spring me from the clutches of "dirty South" justice. Because of Rob's determination, I was out of there before the ink dried. To say that I was elated to not be spending the night in jail would be the understatement of the century. Neither of us could bear the thought of having to explain to our children why Mommy couldn't be home that night.

The next morning, we both woke in a fog. Something akin to a bad hangover. We were sinking into a place where one goes when they come to the realization that things are slowly slipping out of their control. After weeks of unsuccessful negotiations between Rob's defense attorney and special prosecutor Clifford Strider, we were spiritually fatigued and at our wit's end in our efforts to restore the initial plea offer from the state. We'd already been sold up the river by Paul Kidd. Now, to make matters worse, the district attorney brought in Strider, whose track record was less than squeaky clean.[1] The already high stakes were raised yet again. We felt like they were on some kind of evil manhunt. This didn't seem like this was a carrying out of the law or some pursuit of justice—it felt personal.

Not too long after Rob came home on bond, he surprised me in a way I never expected. It was Mother's Day of 1999, and it was an extremely hard season for us. We were working day and night at Culture in the mall but had zero money to do much else other than feed ourselves and the kids and tend to our legal matters. When we got home that Mother's Day evening, Rob handed me a porcelain teddy bear, and inside of the pouch was a beautiful pearl necklace, bracelet, and earrings to match. At first, I wanted to be angry. We didn't have any money for these kinds of extravagances. We were about to go to trial. But I couldn't help but feel so incredibly loved in that moment.

The pearls were the last gift he'd give me before being sent back to prison. They held so much meaning for me. My first strand of pearls was the one my aunt loaned to me when we got married. But now, I had a pair of my own. It was a symbol of our relationship. Pearls are created out of great pressure, great conflict. And yet, they are precious and exemplify class and grace. They come from nothing, but with God's grace and good nature, they become something beautiful, something that stands the test of time.

I've been wearing pearls ever since.

FOX AND ROB

Daily, in courtrooms all across America, young Black men are being hoisted and hung out to die a social death as a result of excessive sentencing. Without delay, Strider went to work, taking all deals off the table and setting Rob and Ontario's trial date.

In May 1999, without adequate counsel, Rob and Ontario were forced to go to trial with a freshman attorney Murphy Bell III, who was straight out of law school with only one trial to his credit. We hired Bell to act temporarily as counsel of record after Kidd walked out on us when the money ran dry. Bell was now being forced to prepare for trial. Within days a lopsided jury comprised of two Blacks and ten whites was selected. The stage had now been set, and the noose affixed. Following the sequestration of the jury, Lincoln Parish district attorney Robert "Bob" Levy entered the courtroom with his family, picnic basket in tow, and ate lunch—in my opinion, salivating in sheer delight—as the rustic reins of justice tightened around our necks. We were breathless. How were we to undo this ever-unfolding injustice? We had no answer. We had no clue.

That's when we sought to take matters into our own hands by sharing information with the only two Black jurors who were on the panel. That too, however, was foiled. The very next day, when we arrived at the courthouse for trial, Fox was accosted outside by both the sheriff and the warden who read her rights, threw her in the back of their police car, and hauled her off to the parish jail. Rob, on the other hand, was immediately rushed by his attorney when he exited the second-floor elevator just outside the courtroom. Screaming at the top of his lungs, Murphy snarled, "What have you all done?! Do you realize how much trouble you are in?!"

Seeing the fear in his eyes, we would have thought that Murphy himself was being charged and arrested. All we knew was that we were facing a lengthy sentence and wanted to do everything in our power to bring justice to ourselves, even if that meant working around a corrupt system. Little did either of us know that jury tampering carries a penalty equal to that of the charge that the jury is impaneled to hear. Armed robbery carries a maximum sentence of 99 years, which means that the two counts of jury tampering that we were now arrested on had us facing a maximum of 297 years behind bars. Despite all, the show went on. In fact, the trial went on until three o'clock the next morning before the jury ended its deliberation. They found both Robert and Ontario guilty as charged.

4

SUBJECT TO THE SYSTEMS THAT SHAPED US

If you are silent about your pain, they'll kill you and say you enjoyed it.

Zora Neale Hurston, *Their Eyes Were Watching God*

FOX AND ROB

We'd done what we felt like we had to do when we robbed that bank. And we were paying handsomely for that crime. A crime that had garnered other people who did not look like us two to seven years or less in the city jail. There was no way to make sense of any of that in the moment though. We just needed to keep working on our freedom. And loving on each other. Now we needed to do everything possible to stabilize our family. But in the midst of all that upheaval, one thing had not changed. The love between us was still palpable. Our physical connection was as passionate as ever. Because of Rob's brief release on bond, we'd just learned that Fox was pregnant.

FOX

Let's go back and revisit the trial and sentencing for a moment. On the first day of Rob's trial in May 1999, I was rearrested, booked into the parish jail, and held on a half million–dollar bond with no clue as to what was happening with Robert and Ontario. I was numb all over. The one thing I knew for certain was that I would be spending my first night in jail. And, despite all the chaos around us, I also knew that God was still looking out for me.

My heart and mind kept returning to the looks on Remington's and Lawrence's faces when they took me in. They had accompanied us to court that day for Rob and Ontario's trial. *How did they know our children would be with us?* Child Protection Services was right there. Waiting on deck to take our sons into custody upon my arrest. I was sick to my stomach. *How heartless could they be?* Not to be forsaken, God showed up in the form of a friend Pam who I knew from Grambling State. She happened to be at the courthouse that morning, and after witnessing the ruckus, came over to see how she could help. Almost on cue, she took the boys and promised to get them safely to my mother, who also had been moved by the Spirit herself that morning. Unbeknownst to me, when Pam reached out to her about delivering the boys, she was already in Ruston, about an hour away from our hometown, Shreveport. Sensing something wasn't right, she'd taken off work that morning and drove to Lincoln Parish to attend the hearing. My mama showed up in the nick of time to get the kids from Pam and out of harm's way.

And there I was in a six-by-nine cell, now facing 297 years behind bars. I was three months pregnant, lying flat on my back, staring at the ceiling, and wondering if I had the strength to carry on. Thinking that I might be suicidal considering how much trouble I was in, the warden ordered his staff to place me in solitary confinement on suicide watch. Now I'd be lying if I didn't admit that I, too, questioned whether I'd be better off dead. But again, in my darkest moment, God showed up. As I lay there, I heard a thump, and then another, and then another. I realized it was the beating of my heart as it pumped blood through my veins. The Holy Spirit spoke to me and reminded me that I had a purpose for being here. That no matter how bad things had gotten, how much had gone afoul in my life, if I was still here, it was for a reason. God was not through with me yet.

And just like a drowning body rescued from troubled waters then resuscitated, I gasped for air. I came to the realization that I was still alive—and that meant something! It meant I needed to get to work to get the hell up out of there and back to my kids.

But where would I begin? After forty-eight hours, the staff realized that I wasn't going to pull the plug on my life, and they placed me in the general population. It wasn't long after I reached the dorm that I received a kite from Rob. A *kite* is a euphemism for a letter exchanged between prisoners. The kite read, *I love you, just thinking of you. Love always, Rob. P.S. See you at yard call.* As always, no matter where we were, we always found a way to stay connected. Prison would be no different.

Later that evening, when I made it to the rec yard, I couldn't help but wonder how Rob was going to reach me. It was against the rules for male and female prisoners to be in any space together. I stood on the stairwell and, to my surprise, heard Rob's voice coming from a second-floor window just above my head. Boy, what a bittersweet delight! Rob had convinced a man two doors down to let him occupy his cell. He then rolled up this brother's mattress and tied it together with the bedsheets so he could stand on top of it in order to be tall enough to talk to me through the window. Now tell me necessity ain't the mother of all invention! This was all very romantic, but knowing the brevity of yard call, Rob and I got down to business. If freedom $= x$, then we needed to solve for it. What would be our order of operations? How could we simplify the magnitude of the problem in which we now found ourselves? Simply put, the strongest thing working for us was that I had an existing health condition. I was three months pregnant and in need of prenatal care, which we knew the parish did not want to shoulder the financial burden of for a pretrial detainee.

The frantic whistle of prison guards pierced our brainstorming session and jarred us back into reality.

"Yard closed!" the big, burly female prison guard yelled. "Catch ya' dorm!"

Looking back on it all, Rob's voice was so comforting to my soul even when heard in the pits of hell. I sullenly returned to the dorm when I heard the same lady hollering out, "Mail call!" My prayers had been answered.

On the home front, Ms. Peggy was furious about the turn

of events. I am certain that if she could have, she would have hung me by my toenails. And can you blame her? I couldn't. Throughout my life, I've certainly acknowledged the impact of my mother's callous ways, but the one reoccurring theme that never fails is that my mother has always shown me that she's got my back. Even when I wasn't at my best self. Concerned about my welfare, my mother called everyone she could think of, namely, she contacted Louisiana congresswoman Mary Landrieu.

As it turned out, the phone calls my mother made had moved heaven and earth for me. Not only had the jail committed to get me to a doctor for my prenatal care but my $500,000 bond had been reduced to $5,000.

Coming through in the direst of circumstances, Ms. Peggy agreed to pull together the $750 needed for me to bond out. The days to follow were torture. The terms of my bond reduction with the DA's office were that they would not hold the hearing until after they had sentenced and shipped Robert and Ontario. We all knew that the sooner I could get my feet back on the ground, the sooner we would get to work at fixing this mess.

"Did you hear?" Rob asked.

The day for Robert and Ontario to be sentenced had finally come. I had been waiting on pins and needles to hear what had happened. I knew that this was about more than the administration of justice. It was about the malicious prosecution of undesirables cloaked in the name of justice. So I waited in angst at what the wrath of their hate would look like in terms of years.

"No. Nobody has told me anything," I responded to Rob while standing in our usual spot at the second-floor window.

"They gave me sixty years, Fox!" Rob spat.

I nearly fainted. By this time, we had learned from my first prenatal care appointment that not only was I pregnant—we had conceived twins. In the midst of this crisis, we went from a family of five to a family of seven! My body was flushed like a burning fire inside. I was sick. In that moment, words from a source greater than me spoke softly through my lips, "Well, it will make the movie mo' better. But I promise we'll walk it together. I won't let go of your hand."

It is important to note that Rob and I have always had plans of one day making a movie. We just never thought it would be a tale about the peculiar ways of the antebellum South. What we discovered on our journey was that these types of happenings were more common than not. Had it not happened to us, never would we have believed that our system was treating human beings in this manner. People are not chattel, and they shouldn't be treated as such. Even if they have broken societal codes of conduct, they remain human.

FOX AND ROB

After an eventful trial in May of 1999, Rob and Ontario were tried, convicted, and subsequently sentenced to serve sixty and forty-five years, respectively, without the benefit of probation, parole, or suspension of sentence. Within days, they were transported to Angola State Penitentiary, where the two of them immediately began their lengthy appellate process.

On July 4, 1999, Fox walked out of Lincoln Parish Detention Center on bond, emotionally and spiritually battered and bruised. It had been an exhausting two years, but on the sixty-mile drive back to Shreveport, she came to the realization that serving time for her was basically inevitable. So she immediately began to inform key members of the community of her untimely departure. While out on bond, Fox ran Culture, which had already been reduced to a corner store and antiques shop under her mother's leadership, in order to keep some change in her pocket until she left for prison. At which time we shut down the entire operation. Fox's mother could not keep all our kids, teach school, and run the shop too.

Fox, after much negotiating back and forth, agreed to take a plea deal for two seven-year sentences and one five-year sentence, all running concurrently. All of this was only after giving birth to twin boys, Freedom and Justus, just ten months prior. And now, with five children between us, Fox was faced with leaving the babies and our business to serve her time.

FOX

On the same morning I was sentenced, August 31, 2000, I had to be at the hospital at five o'clock in the morning. Our son Freedom was born with extra digits, and the doctors felt like it would be socially unacceptable for him to proceed in life that way. My mother was with me and had agreed to keep my babies while I did my time. That was a hard decision for both of us. Mama was enraged, and possibly even heartbroken. How could I have even put myself in that situation? And, I have to admit, I was anxious about leaving my children with her. *How could I have done this to our children?* I thought.

It was my responsibility to raise them, not my mother's. But what choice did I have?

Freedom, only ten months old at the time, was crying so hard that day. Wailing, almost. Mostly because he was hungry and couldn't eat before the surgery. But I can't help but wonder if he sensed that I was going away. I'll never actually know, but it's something I do think about. When I kissed my baby before he headed into the operating room, I wasn't just saying bye for a few hours. When he came out of surgery, his mother would be gone. For a long time.

That hurt.

But I was doing my best with the circumstances I found myself in. I stayed with Freedom as the nurses readied him for surgery. I tried to show my mother as much affection as she would allow me. Then at 7:00 a.m., I left the hospital with my self-appointed godfather Frank, a Vietnam vet who had given me the wisdom not to run when I was considering the option of jumping my half million–dollar bond and living on the run. He was driving me to court so I could turn myself in for sentencing. I knew I was going to be remanded to the custody of the Louisiana Department of Corrections, so Frank was going to take my car back to Shreveport and gift it to Ms. Wanda, an elder in my community who had committed to helping my mother by babysitting the boys. This way, my mother could continue to teach while she cared for them.

But even prior to that day, I'd spent that entire summer with my boys, trying to make sure they had clear memories of joy and love with their mother. That was incredibly important to me. I also tried my best to make as many contacts as I could. In fact, I basically went to everybody in my community and told them that I was accepting the plea deal that was offered to me at the beginning of July, and I needed a village to look out for my boys. I couldn't risk a trial and the potential for the forty years they had initially offered. I'd already seen how the system had thrown Robert and Ontario away. I didn't want to be made another example.

I didn't even know anything about the forty-year offer at first. My attorney only shared that with me when I balked at the twelve years they ended up offering me in the deal. If I accepted twelve, then I could serve six years and be released on good behavior. The biggest problem I had with the deal was that it was a sentence that offered no right to parole. In Louisiana at that time, a first offender was automatically given the right to parole, unless they took a plea deal that removed that opportunity. My attorney, on the other hand, thought the twelve years was a far cry from the forty and an option I should consider.

"I'm just telling you what your options are," he said.

I had to decide. But I also needed and wanted to sleep on it. I was thinking, *I'm twenty-eight years old and just gave birth to twins who are not even a year old yet. If I'm gone for six years, my babies will be in second grade before they see their mother. That's bad enough. But it's still a hell of a difference from returning to them when they are in their forties.* Nevertheless, that feeling I often get of being out of my body had returned. It was like I was watching myself wrestle with this decision. My mother tried to assure me that everything would be alright.

"Now Sibil, you go on and do what you got to do to get this behind you. Me and those boys are going to be alright," she said.

How do I do this?

Her words were like body blows. I'd spent so much time focused on having to go to prison that it was just dawning on me that my absence was going to have a considerable impact on my boys. Everything got real.

If there's one thing I know, I was and am a good mother. I may not have been good at much else, and maybe I didn't always make the best decisions, but I love those boys with every fiber of my being. And even to this day, with all due respect, I strive to be twice the mother my mother was able to be to me. I'm really grateful for my mother and her example of always doing what was necessary to keep her children clothed, fed, and educated. So that body blow I took when she said "those boys are going to be alright" was more about feeling like I'd forfeited my responsibility of mothering my children the way I had wanted to, the way they needed. I was going to have to entrust their little hearts to someone other than myself.

The next morning, less than twenty-four hours after talking with my attorney and wrestling with the implications of accepting the plea deal, I woke up prepared to talk to my oldest son Remington, who was six, about the latest developments. It was a hot, muggy summer morning when he and I left the house for a walk in Veteran's Park, one of our favorite hangouts. This talk clearly reigns as one of the most painful conversations I have ever had to have in my life. Over the years, Remi and I had weathered plenty of storms together, but nothing like this. Along the path I found a stopping point and bent down so that I could look him in his eyes. Then I said, "They are making me go to prison. So I am going to have to leave, baby."

"Nooooo!" He screamed at the top of his lungs with tears

pouring from his eyes. "I thought you said when Daddy left, you weren't gonna have to leave."

I wrapped him in my arms and said, "I know! But they are making me go, and the sooner I go, the sooner I can get back home to you."

We held each other tight for what seemed like an eternity. After he had gotten it all out, we both wiped our tears away and began the journey back home. In my lifetime, I have learned that one of the most valuable things any of us can give to our children is the truth. Even when it hurts like hell.

ROB

I can only imagine how hard that conversation must have been for Fox to have with Remi. Beyond hard. It was one thing for us to accept responsibility for wrongdoing, but this was another thing altogether. When considering Fox's limited role in all of this, forcing her to go to prison made a terrible situation so much worse. In my efforts to protect myself from all the emotions that were building up inside me, I shut down some. I know in hindsight that I probably wasn't as sensitive to Fox's feelings at the time. The truth is, I couldn't allow myself to feel the pain. I chose to focus on the work. My family's restoration. My appeal. Hell, my escape if it came to that. When Fox and I did get an opportunity to speak via phone or in person, which wasn't very often because of her case, we never really talked about the emotional and psychological impact of what was happening to our family. All the ways we were being torn apart. We couldn't. It was too much. We simply tried to give each other words of empowerment. We encouraged each other.

She didn't tell me about the hardships she was facing. She didn't express anything about how she was feeling as much as she tried to just keep my spirits up. And it was the same for me. I never really talked much about what I was witnessing or experiencing in prison because I didn't want to burden her any further. I think this was our way of coping. We knew we needed to have a tough layer of skin to deal with what was coming, for however long it was going to be. That hardness was the only way we were going to endure it.

When I think about it now, I realize that disengaging in this way was how I protected my heart. How could I hold the pain of leaving my sons? Not just the four boys I had with Fox but also my son Mahlik, who lived in New Jersey with his mom. Prior to Fox and me getting married, his mom and I were together during the early years of his life. I'd been an active father for Mahlik's first year, doing all the things that daddies do and then some. I'd tasted fatherhood and loved it. And now I was acutely aware that I'd left my children socially orphaned.

Deep down inside I believed that I was a good person and had been working every day to prove that. It was one of the reasons why I asked for Fox's hand in marriage. I was trying to right some of the wrongs of my life. I was trying to somehow be a better demonstration of what manhood could look like. Instead, I felt boxed in by my life but was determined to break free. But it turned out, I still couldn't get it right. Sixty years in prison. My nephew, whose care I had been entrusted with by my sister because he was already getting into trouble in Kansas City where he was from, was now sentenced to forty-five years in prison for assisting me in this crime. I was supposed to help him get on the right path, and I'd led him down the wrong one. The burden of it all weighed heavy on my soul.

All I could hear as the judge explained his sentence for me was my failure. Judge Wayne Smith called me the "mastermind" during the sentencing. He didn't see my ambition, as misguided as it may have been. He didn't understand anything about the American Dream Syndrome and how it impacts the thinking of go-getters, even if it didn't justify my actions. He didn't see that I was salvageable. He chose not to see my humanity. Otherwise, how could he have concluded that a sixty- and forty-five-year sentence, respectively, as first offenders was just? He simply said that I was the oldest of the three of us and should have known better. And I suppose, in an unsettling way, I felt that to be true. That part stuck with me. I should have known better.

In my mind, how *could* I hold all the heavy emotions that would rise up in me when I thought about how the terrible choice we made that day had stolen my ability to love who I loved in the way they deserved? It would have consumed me.

So, I didn't hold them at all. I couldn't. I chose hope, but not simply for the sake of empty optimism. I chose faith. I trusted that God would see me through. Even if I didn't know how.

The last time we were physically together, Fox and I were joined by our lawyer who informed us that we were each facing 297 years apiece. At that time, I gave Fox the greatest words I could muster up in the moment. Words I hoped would bring her some comfort. Words I'd been speaking to myself in order to find some peace in the midst of this storm.

"Despite all we are going through, we are going to be alright."

FOX

Can you believe it? With all that was going on, this man had the spiritual resolve to tell me, "Everything was going to be alright."

And I believed him. I had to.

Choosing to speak life over one another was certainly a survival mechanism. We could have allowed ourselves to be consumed by the traumatic nature of our experience, but we didn't. Despite the pain that was right on the surface, we suppressed it all so that we could live through what would ultimately be twenty-one years of separation. We're not saying it was healthy; we're saying it was the only way we knew how to cope at the time. How would we be able to do the research we needed to unpack Louisiana's unjust and unfair laws around sentencing, or even show up for our children in whatever capacity we could, if we were always stuck in a quagmire emotionally? That wasn't going to work.

ROB

I don't care what anyone says, or how it's portrayed in the latest song or popular TV crime drama, when you are jailed, you feel like an animal being caged. Your emotions run wild, and the bondage affects not only your body but your mind and your spirit. It's a system that is designed to syphon away your humanity. When I first went to Angola, all I could think about was getting out by any and all means necessary. My soul was heavy with grief and agony. So I was grateful when I encountered a gentleman who helped give me some perspective. He was steeped in Louisiana law and urged me to attend the weekly law class being held in the main prison education building. Lamont Mathews was a Houston native sentenced to life in prison. He was a warm, gentle spirit, wise beyond his years, who offered me sage advice on how best to navigate Louisiana's criminal justice system. He began by telling me I first must outlive my oppressor. Hence, I needed to work out and keep my body in shape. He went on to say, "Prison is an emotionally charged environment and you must curb your emotions if you hope to ever be able to get through this." He said if I approached the situation I was in with the levels of extreme emotion I was feeling, it would cloud my better judgment and I'd start to make choices that would not help my matter. In fact, those choices could lead me even deeper into the pits of hell.

So, I continued to numb myself.

FOX

We both numbed ourselves. We didn't know any other way to navigate the system we were now subjects in. There were no lessons available about empathy and self-compassion in the midst of trials so great. And this was especially true for me. There's this strong Black woman trope that hovers over every Black woman we know. This idea that they aren't allowed to be soft or gentle or outwardly acknowledge or express pain. As Zora Neale Hurston writes in her seminal novel *Their Eyes Were Watching God*, Black women are the mules of the earth, and it's so easy to buy into that perception.[1] Black women can sometimes carry strength like a badge of honor and never allow their hearts to be tended to in the way that's really needed. Unfortunately, that stance, as valid and necessary a posture as it seems to be, can feed the dehumanization that Black women face on a near daily basis. Black women don't get to scream and cry. Fragility isn't afforded them. They push the pain down and power through. And they pay the price for it.

Not being able to really express the emotional aspect of what we were going through was not healthy for me in the long run. In many ways, it fueled an anger that seemed to burn just under the surface for me. There were so many times, even after my release, when people would say, "Fox, why are you going from zero to one hundred?" about something they perceived as a minor slight or problem. What they didn't understand is that I wasn't going from zero to one hundred. I didn't even know what zero looked like. Internally, I hung out at 99.5, so getting to one hundred was quite easy.

It's something I still wrestle with, but with prayer and meditation, I am getting better. Everything was intensified because of the depth of my long suffering. I could never find a release valve, and as a Black woman, I wasn't really allowed one.

So, all that sorrow and pain and guilt and anxiety and anguish just plugged up my soul. And like weeds in a field full of flowers, it grew and choked out the good. It consumed me to the point where, yes, I finally released it, but in all the wrong and harmful ways. I would spew that pain out on the customer service agent. On my children. On my family and friends.

And that's when I fell into the trap of another horrible

trope—the angry Black woman. Isn't that something? We aren't allowed the space to grieve and express our pain. We aren't given any room to be vulnerable without repercussions. In some cases, there's no one there to hold us and allow us to scream and cry without judging that sound and those tears. So, we keep it in, and when it overtakes us to the point where we feel like we'll die if we don't release it, we are labeled as angry and put into another box. Hell yes, I'm angry! I'm human. I can't hold it all, even when I try. There were so many moments right before I was sentenced, and even after I was released, when all I wanted was to be held. As human beings, our bodies are designed for connection. We have the capacity to heal and reconcile, often with just the power of a hug or smile or listening ear. But for me as a Black woman, that can often feel so foreign. Fifty years of living with constant and regular dehumanization, subtle or overt, means that I am only now trying to find healthy ways to move some of this pain out of my body. It's been hard to even get Rob to understand that. To help me with that.

ROB

I know. Vulnerability is still a challenge for me. I've had twenty years of practice at keeping my emotions at bay in order to survive every single day in the penitentiary. In order to keep the institutionalization that the system wanted for me at bay. So it takes time to unravel from that.

I also think that part of it is probably the way men and women of my generation were raised. Especially in the South. At least in the framework that I had been brought up under, boys were taught to be tough. We were taught to never express our emotions lest we be considered weak. Doing so meant that we were soft and ripe for aggression. So, I suppose long before I ever went to prison, I'd created this way of coping and dealing with grief that pushed down my pain. This was especially true after losing my mother at the age of five. After all, nurturing fathers were not a thing where I was from in the 1970s. My dad, like most men of his era, taught you how to fend for yourself, keep your word, and work hard for the things you wanted in life. Hold all those emotions. Needless to say, with the loss of my mother, my kindergarten years were set up a little differently than my peers'.

It was a pattern in my family. To not talk about the things that hurt. In this instance, no one ever really sat me down and talked about where people transitioned to after death. At such a young age, I couldn't understand fully what had happened to my mother at death. So, I drew my own conclusions—as much as a little kid could. I remember my mother telling me that my name, Robert, meant "Lord." When I attended my mother's funeral and heard the eulogist saying something like "Sister Fannie Mae has gone home to be with the *Lord*," I believed for the longest time that my mom had abandoned us for another Robert. Crazy, right? To think that most people aren't given any guidance or framework for processing grief but are given plenty of reasons why openly expressing it is not acceptable—especially for a man. Over time, pushing away hard emotions became my modus operandi. I didn't tap in. Nor did I wear my feelings on my sleeve. I couldn't. I just held it all in until I reached a breaking point and would then explode.

I don't say any of this as an excuse. Clearly, Fox needed

me emotionally in ways I couldn't understand. I suppose I *am* saying that living most of my life without the nurturing of my mother informed how I moved through the world and how I approached relationships. And being imprisoned for over twenty years surely didn't make any of that easier. I've grown up with this seemingly permanent bend in my life as to how I address trauma and hardship. Sometimes it makes me come off as heartless; I know that now. And I do long for the day I can truly tap into that level of emotional freedom. Surely, it's got to be liberating.

FOX AND ROB

There's enough science available to us now that shows how trauma can be trapped in our bodies. It's the way God designed our bodies to work. When we are faced with a traumatic experience, our bodies move into fight, flight, or freeze mode to keep us safe. The challenge with this is that sometimes, if we don't address what's happening, we can get stuck in one of these modes. Our bodies, when seemingly triggered, will perpetually act in the same ways they always have to make sense of what's happening and/or to keep us safe. Doesn't really matter if the threat is real or even the same as before. The past is the present as far as our bodies and brains are concerned. *We* have to tell them otherwise.

Black people intuitively know this better than most. As a result of white supremacist institutions and regular encounters with both subtle and overt forms of racism, we often walk around in a hypervigilant state. Just like other forms of trauma, racial trauma can live in the body; and just like Rob, we can find ourselves holding on to the pain so tightly that it begins to affect everything and everyone around us. But the hard truth is that pain is going to come out at some point. It has to. The questions are when, where, and how.

Part of the healing journey for both of us has been about doing our best to make space for each other's vulnerability. But also making sure we stay grounded together in the things that matter. We pray together and dream together. We do our social justice work with an eye on helping other families begin their own journey toward healing. Rob knows now that it is important to make sure Fox feels like she can put down her armor and be vulnerable. That his comfort and covering will always be available to her. Fox knows now the source of Rob's discomfort around expressing emotions and can offer grace to him in the moments when some of those old patterns show up. We can unbend ourselves from all the ways we've been contorted and shaped into something that doesn't fit our destiny.

5

THE EXCEPTION

What lies behind of us and what lies before us are tiny matters compared to what lives within us.

Henry Stanley Haskins, *Meditations in Wall Street*

FOX AND ROB

Slavery was abolished in the United States in 1865 by the ratification of the thirteenth amendment—"except as a punishment for crime." With all of us now behind prison bars, it was official: we had hit rock bottom. We were enslaved. Making a mockery of Rob's sentence, Clifford R. Strider III, special prosecutor for the state, told him in a sidebar that he received sixty-one years as a kind of reminder. That one extra year was significant to him. It was a reminder that the last time someone committed jury tampering in Ruston was in 1938. Rob was sentenced in 1999. He received sixty years for the armed robbery and one year for jury tampering to be run consecutively. Giving him a sixty-one-year sentence. The exact number of years from 1938 to 1999.

To us, Strider was a prosecutorial zealot whose actions made it seem like he believed that all defendants are guilty of something and deserve maximum penalties. Hence, we were no different than the countless others who were subject to those actions. But you see, truth be told, we are our own kind of fanatics as well. We are fanatical about this love. We are fanatical about this family. We are fanatical about success and the realization of our dreams. And in response to Rob's sentencing, we were more committed than ever before to not take that licking lying down. This was a clash of wills. A contest in which each side was determined to get what it wanted and neither side was willing to yield or compromise. The state wanted death. And we wanted what God had promised us—life, more abundantly. And what God had given, we would never stop fighting for.

FOX

Almost three years from when this tragedy started, to the date, I was transported to the prison where I would serve my time. I couldn't have prepared myself for what I saw when I arrived at Richland Parish Detention Center in September 2000. Like most, I had seen prison life on television, and was frankly scared of the violent culture I might encounter. Fear aside, I knew that they had given me a substantial amount of time. I decided early on to make it work for me and not against me. When I returned home to my family, I had to be a better version of myself. Rob had told me about the training programs they had at Angola, and that part I was looking forward to. Whatever good I could take away from this enormous tragedy, so be it.

Boy, was I wrong.

Part of what I witnessed in this prison where cotton was once king and the plantation owners worked captives from *can't see to can't see* was a sheriff managing a similar commodity. What commodity? You guessed it—Black and Brown bodies. This place was a *lock and feed*. I had heard about how prisons are no longer about rehabilitation but about the warehousing of human beings. When I stepped foot into the three thousand-plus square-foot open dormitory, it was as though I had walked into a time warp.

At Richland Parish Detention Center, seventy-five women were locked up per warehouse with only eight open toilets and eight open showers for all of us. We publicly used the restroom where all others gathered, communed, and slept. There were no guards inside the room. Security sat outside of the dormitory, looking at us through Plexiglas as if we were animals in a zoo. It was such an inhumane thing to live through. I mean, there was one time when the tap water was green! They kept telling us that the water was okay, but it was green.

There were no programs, and there weren't even any windows. We were only allowed to go to chow three times a day, walking in a straight line with our hands behind our back, and had only three required hours of weekly outdoor recreation. The room coined as *the library* was only filled with murder mystery novels—imagine that.

What happened to education? The training? I know they've got something for us to do here.

They did have one club there, and it was a choir who would travel locally to sing for churches in the small town. They also had a weekly GED class that the teacher (another small-town local who was related to the warden) never seemed to make it to. And if she didn't come, there was no class, and that was extremely unfortunate. Because even if the women wanted to better themselves, there was no computer access and no consistent training.

Not to mention that the only work available, if you could get it, was menial. There were only twelve jobs available for over one thousand or so women who were housed at this facility. One could work in the kitchen or as a hall monitor, but if you weren't one of those twelve, you had literally nothing to do all day. Nothing at all for these women, some of whom had been sentenced to decades of time. I watched many of them sleep their time away. This was not going to be my story. If I was going to use this time for the betterment of me, I had to figure it out.

Like Jesus in Matthew 21:10, I wanted my presence to have an impact in that wretched place. My hope was to bring light to where there was darkness. After my first few nights in prison, knowing that my intentions were to use my voice to speak for the voiceless upon my release, I made my first speech.

I remembered the words of Dr. Wayne Dyer, "Anything you are ever going to be, you are it already."[1] I was a motivational speaker. The revelation of this truth became clear to me in

1996 after reading Les Brown's book *Live Your Dreams*[2]—
and this was certainly mine. So, I spoke. God knows, if anyone needed an uplifting word, it was me and the seventy-four
other women in Dorm 4 on that night. It was a Sunday evening; I stood up on my bunk and grabbed everyone's attention. I shared with them that I was a motivational speaker on
the streets, and I felt like we all could use a revival. I delivered
a message based on the story of Humpty-Dumpty and how
no one could put him back together again after his great fall.
My lecture was to remind my sisters that, unlike Humpty-
Dumpty, God was our maker. And with God, all things were
and are possible—including the possibility of our lives being
put back together again. It was pretty bold when I consider
this now. A new girl in the joint, directing these women to see
beyond their current situation and continue holding a vision
for their future? But that is what the power of God does. It
emboldens you.

It never fails. Light allowed in any room pushes darkness
back into the corners. I witnessed a spark over those next
few days. A quickening of the spirit and a touch of light
radiated from many of the women.

By 2001, I was finding my rhythm and making things happen right where I was. I started writing a book to talk about
what life looked like behind prison walls. I wrote the book for
myself and for those women. I thought that if people knew
about what was happening, then maybe we would make different choices. Or maybe the systems would be shamed into
offering something that would actually facilitate rehabilitation. I thought I could make a difference, but I was especially
conscious of not pissing off the administration.

What does the system hate more than a prisoner who

reads? One who writes. Because the system can't stand it when the oppressed access their most powerful force—their voice.

In fact, when they found out I was writing a book, they shipped me to three different prisons. Moving from prison to prison is another traumatic experience because they come and get you in the middle of the night. They grab you; make you throw all your belongings and personal items into big black trash bags; and force you to lug them to the next place. You don't know where you're going until you get there. There's no way to alert your family. And when you get there—to yet another poverty-stricken small town in the deep woods of Louisiana—they all but drop you off on the curb and process you into a new prison.

Rumors of me working on a book landed me in Avoyelles's Parish Prison. There I would meet Mr. Rufus C. Johnson, head of the GED program. Unlike the other leaders in the institutions where I had been housed, he was committed to helping the women in his program get an education. Always seeking the next opportunity, I convinced him to hire me as his head tutor. Meanwhile from Angola, Rob found out that IMPACT at Louisiana Correctional Institute for Women (LCIW) was a way I could return home sooner. I could apply to the six-month boot camp and then be released to complete the remainder of my sentence at home under supervision. Empowered with that information, I went to work writing the warden, requesting she ship me for those reasons—all to no avail. At my wit's end, I begged Mr. Johnson to help me get moved to LCIW to get into their program and return expeditiously to my children. Being a devout family man himself, he gave me his word he would try.

It worked! Less than thirty days later, I was shipped to the women's prison where I awaited acceptance. A small victory but a victory, no doubt.

Louisiana Correctional Institute for Women, located in Saint Gabriel, Louisiana, was responsible for housing the most violent and longest-serving women in our state. But if being there meant getting back home to my children sooner, I was willing. The next step was figuring out how to get into the program.

As soon as my feet hit the campus, I started asking anyone and everyone about the boot camp. Most participants were there by court order, but anyone could apply nonetheless, just as Rob researched. I wrote to the person in charge of the program and applied. The security officers around me told me they thought I was a perfect candidate and were optimistic with me about my chances of getting in. I met the criteria—a sentence of no more than seven years and a first-time, nonviolent offender. They had to accept me! I was a shoo-in, right?

Apparently not. *I was denied!*

Without explanation, I was turned down. According to the law, I qualified, so I will never know why those in charge did not see me as someone ripe for this program. That moment made me feel like there were some unseen forces out there working against me. But I had no time for witch hunts or conspiracy theories. When someone has fallen as far in life as we had, they have to always see the glass as half *full*. I wiped away the tears and started looking for the silver lining in all of this. From that point forward, I saw this institution as just another stop on my tour through this peculiar system.

Making it to the state-run women's prison was certainly

a step in the right direction. They had programming and offered a chance to be sent to work release. At work release, you could earn money for your labor—albeit four cents an hour—before returning home instead of working for free like in the sheriff-run facilities. Being able to make some money was important for women like me who were returning citizens with little to no available resources upon release. When you factor in that 80 percent of women released have children to care for, it makes the practice of this catch-and-release system of serfdom all the more harmful.

Nevertheless, my time at LCIW hit a little different. I joined Toastmasters, which helped me continue to refine my speaking craft, and I went on tour within the prison, speaking to the various clubs, classes, and organizations. I graduated from a computer class, and even had the opportunity to open Christmas presents with my boys (thanks to the Angel Tree organization). Through the LCIW parenting program, I was afforded time with the boys, who were allowed to visit on the grounds of the compound—by far one of the few humanizing experiences I had while incarcerated. Once every three months, my sons had a chance to not only come on-site, but they could also visit with me in the dorm room I shared with one other young lady. Oh my, we would play on the swing set, roll around on the grass, play tag, eat in the dining hall, and snack out of my locker box that I was all too excited to fill with goodies in anticipation of their arrival! This act of kindness brought ease to my boys and allowed them to rest, knowing that their mother was safe and unbroken.

My next challenge? Work release. Going home to four of our five children, I had to earn some money. It wasn't an option; it was a necessity. There's no way I could go home as a burden on my family. Once eligible, I had to get to the top of the long waiting list. A cousin I grew up with had a friend at the Department of Corrections and said she would see if she could get me pulled to go to a halfway house.

Again, it worked! I was about to spend my last days behind bars. *Praise God!*

There weren't that many beds at the halfway houses for women, so the competition was stiff, and if you messed up at work release, you got shipped back to the prison—no questions asked. Talk about a walk of shame! So, I had to tread lightly.

It was January 3, 2002, and my name came out on the list! I was headed to Lake Charles halfway house. *Oh no!* I'd heard that this particular place was hell, and I was about to find out just how much. But anything would be better than prison. The director picked up about six of us from the prison and drove almost three hours to Lake Charles. The next morning, I discovered our jobs were already assigned. We were sent to work in housekeeping at a Holiday Inn in Sulfur, Louisiana, that catered to contracted plant workers. Cleaning hotel rooms with a master's degree was quite humbling, to say the least. But I was willing to do whatever I had to do and leaned into the words of Dr. Martin Luther King Jr. who once said if you are going to be a street sweeper, be the best street sweeper.[3] I was a housekeeper with two degrees, and my rooms were a reflection of me. They were spotless. I was going to be the best housekeeper I could be. And trust, cleaning up behind workers at a sulfur plant took real commitment. But I was still hopeful to have a better paying position, even if it was at the same hotel. After about a week or so of drop-offs and pickups, I discovered that one of the other residents at the halfway house was a shift manager at the Burger King in front of the Holiday Inn. She told me they were hiring another shift manager. The next day, when we were picking her up, I hopped off the transport bus and went in asking the manager Mrs. June for the job. It would double the minimum wage of $5.25 I was making at the hotel. And I would have access to a computer to write and a phone so I could call my boys.

At every turn, I kept discovering that, when I was willing, God never made it as hard on me as it could have been. I moved with greater ease just because I was willing to do the next right thing. It had taken a long time for me to get to that space, but once I was there, there was no turning back.

As much as the director at the halfway house didn't want me to change jobs, she couldn't justify making me stay at a job that paid less. But she surely tried—which didn't make sense considering the halfway house makes half of whatever we make. The more I made, the more they made.

Every morning, before my shift, I showed up at the store at three so I could squeeze in some time to write before I opened the restaurant. One day, Laurence Morrow, the owner of the Lake Charles newspaper *Gumbeaux Magazine*, stopped in. I had been reading the paper and shared with him that I used to write a weekly column for the *Shreveport Times*, and I was interested in writing for him. He welcomed the idea, and I was on to the next opportunity. At least until things went left again.

Things were going well for about the first month, but then security showed up one day and pulled me off my job. When that happened, I knew I was in some trouble. I may as well pack my bags because I figured I was headed back to the slammer. My mouth went dry. *What did I do?* When I got back to the house, the directors were waiting on me.

"Do you remember how you told us you wanted to go to the other halfway house in Monroe so you could go to school? We made that happen for you. We do not appreciate you writing in the local newspapers, so we think it's best for all parties involved to move you to another facility."

I was speechless, but I wouldn't dare look the gift horse in the mouth, not even in gratitude. The City of Faith halfway house was in North Louisiana! I would be closer to home and to my boys. Plus, it was a facility that allowed me to work outside of the companies they contracted for labor. And there were weekend furloughs!

I arrived at the City of Faith in June 2002. It was so surreal. The property was immaculate, and most importantly, peaceful. My first interaction was with their director, who summoned me to his office the second I arrived. He wanted to see who the secretary of the Department of Corrections had called in a favor for.

"Let's be clear," he said. "They never transfer prisoners between work release programs. There must be something special about you."

I thought to myself, *Favor ain't fair.*

And favor is what I experienced as I got closer to the home stretch of my journey inside the prison system. In Monroe, I landed a job as the public relations director for one of the largest nonprofits in the area, founded by community leader Esther Gallow. I admired her so much, I adopted her as my godmother. Having spent the last year of my sentence at work release, I was positioned for a strong return home.

ROB

I could hear the eerie sounds of shackles and chains approaching in the distance from where I woke suddenly in my cell. The clanking of the leg irons sent chills up my spine. It was as though the DNA of castaways from centuries ago had awakened in me. The hair stood up on my neck. My shoulders tightened. I felt what some may describe as a PTSD flashback. I was shook! Then a tall, lanky, grimacing old guard appeared out of the dark of night, and in an instant, I was Angola bound.

On August 7, 1999, I entered the gates of Angola State Penitentiary. The 250-mile ride from northwest Louisiana to the prison was quite sobering, to say the least. It was muggy and hot aboard the ghostly, modified, fifty-passenger school bus. An occasional breeze crept through the open windows covered in chicken wire. The journey started with a handful of men and grew exponentially as we stopped at various institutions along the way. Each stop was like a condemned persons depot. We were loaded and unloaded like livestock. This was a lot to take in. But now wasn't the time to let it all penetrate. I had other things on my mind.

Back home, members of my family had started bad-mouthing Fox about the robbery, and it bothered me because I was not there to confront them. I thought tragedy was supposed to bring families closer together, but what I witnessed was a further divide. Truth be told, I guess we all needed someone to blame. Feels better that way, right? It has been a long-standing view on both sides of our families that when Fox and I come together, we have this fiery thing that is explosive in very good and not so good ways. We are unabashedly driven, and our passion for each other and our dreams run deep. Both of these things made people in our immediate circle extremely uncomfortable. That kind of untamed love and lofty ambition was not familiar to them, especially below the Mason-Dixon Line where so many of our ideas were unacceptable and frowned upon. We were a part of a minority group of early adapters who envisioned new wave products and services for us, by us, in the spirit of FUBU. The thought of all of that spooked those around us.

At the onset of all of this, I blamed both family and friends for not investing in *my* dreams of opening an urban clothing store. I mean, had they given me the money I wouldn't have had to rob a bank. I blamed the mothers of my unplanned children, both Mahlik's mother in New Jersey and Fox. After all, thanks to them, I dropped out of college that year to be a daddy. That had to have contributed to my downfall, right? I blamed the media for putting out films like *Point Break*, *Dead Prez*, and *Set It Off*—films that enticed countless Gen Xers to choose quick fixes to big and seemingly overwhelming problems. I blamed the culture for making the delinquent behavior of these young men and women not only socially acceptable, but en vogue. I even blamed myself for turning right instead of left when I exited the bank that day. And, of course, worst of all, I blamed God. Because surely he had to have seen all of this coming. In my mind, at that moment, there was enough blame to go around.

But I soon came to realize that blaming others was not going to fix our problems. We were clearly going to have to carry our own water. Instead of trying to solve our family feuds, we chose to move in the direction of acceptance. One of my brothers reportedly said that "if Robert is smart enough to get himself into trouble then he should be smart enough to get himself out." Although it hurt, I never held that statement to heart. I had already died to what once had me bound and I ought to serve in the new way of the Spirit, as Romans 7:6 teaches. Therefore, I accepted his harsh words as they mirrored something else, something I once read regarding the most powerful two-letter words in a sentence: "If it is to be, it is to be by me." Simply put, if I was going to be delivered from bondage, I needed to skip the passive-aggressive infighting and get to work.

The sound of screeching tires against the asphalt broke the silence as our transport vehicle veered to the right and pulled through a gate into a parking lot. The driver put the bus in park, and you could hear and feel the exhalation of the hydraulic brakes as the pressure released.

"Welcome home, ladies," the armed guard greeted us as we were all told to unload.

Almost without thinking, we formed a line. Inmates and guards alike gathered around, looking us over as if they all were inspecting precious cargo. After standing in formation and in the sweltering heat for what seemed like an eternity, we were herded into the receiving center building. RC, as the building was affectionately known, also housed death row inmates. Once inside, we were further humiliated. Our heads were shaved bald, our bodies doused in lye, and our personal effects trashed and later claimed by other offenders working on-site. Needless to say, I was exhausted and wanted nothing more than for this to be over. I was disgusted and sick in my stomach. I needed to lay down. Sleep it off a bit.

"Count clear!" an officer yelled.

With my dorm assignment and other pertinent items in hand, I headed to Hickory-3, bed 57, Main Prison West Yard. By the time I made it to the dorm, lights were out, and it had to be well after ten at night. I stopped at the security desk for directions and, like a blind man, felt my way to my rack. I dumped my stuff on the floor in the aisle and collapsed on the bed beneath me. I heard others breathing, although I couldn't see them. With my eyes finally adjusting to the darkness, I realized that there were countless bodies covered in white sheets sprawled across the dormitory in a head to toe, zigzag fashion. It looked like the graphic images of slaves in the hull of a ship.

What I wouldn't do to hear Fox's voice right now.

In a dorm full of men, I felt so alone. The coming months were tough. Because of the distance, lack of money, and unreliable transportation, visits from Fox and the boys were few and far between. *What will this type of strain do to our relationship?*

News of Fox's departure to prison was bittersweet. I knew that the sooner she could get shipped, the sooner she could return to our boys who were growing rapidly with each passing day. I soon found my rhythm in the drudgery of prison life. I joined the ranks of two organizations focused on parole eligibility for lifers. The Angola Special Civics Project (ASCP) and Lifers. The programs were led by long-serving offenders who shared the history and wealth of their failed appellate attempts. By November 2000, my direct appeal to the Louisiana Supreme Court was denied. There I was, four years in, and I was now mounting my own history of failed attempts.

Romans 7:24 resonated in my mind, "What a wretched man I am! Who will rescue me from this body that is subject to death?"

FOX AND ROB

When it all falls down, so much is revealed. Booker T. Washington said it best: "Success is measured not so much by the position that one has reached in life as by the obstacles which he has overcome."[4] Despite our meager and humble beginnings, neither of us comes from families steeped in a life of crime. Therefore, being drug through the halls of justice and running back and forth to prison facilities to care for a loved one has never been a part of our families' culture. To their credit, they did what they knew best. They prayed. We, on the other hand, did what we do best. We rose to the challenge. God had chosen us for this defining moment in time.

6

A FAMILY REUNION

I am no longer accepting the things I cannot change. I am changing the things I cannot accept.

Angela Y. Davis

FOX AND ROB

The days leading up to Fox's release from incarceration were filled with uncertainty. She'd spent nearly a year living in City of Faith halfway house in Monroe. With every sunrise and sunset, the intensity of what was happening settled in. Would they really let her leave? Or would they find another reason to hold her longer? To keep her from her babies?

Fortunately, on October 23, 2002, at 8:00 a.m., they did

not stop Fox from finally leaving the custody of the state. Between her good time credits and her educational credits for programs she'd completed, Fox was granted release.

FOX

It's a day I will never, ever forget. I packed up everything I had, which wasn't much. I had the clothes on my back and a 1978 mint-green Buick LeSabre that I had purchased from the halfway house administrators. It was affectionately known by the boys and me as the green machine. Man, I was gassed up and ready to go! But they wouldn't let me pull off until exactly 8:00 a.m. So, I sat in the car and waited. Those minutes ticked by like a bomb about to explode, except the only thing that was going to go off that day was me! I had a place lined up. And my first stop was to pick up my babies. The twins were now three; Lawrence, six; and Remington, nine. During my time away, I may have been fortunate enough to see my sons every ninety days, if resources permitted. God knows I missed them.

When the clock struck eight and I realized that regaining my freedom was inevitable, I put that green machine in reverse and took a selfie as I was leaving. I felt like Tupac, "Picture Me Rollin'."[1]

"I'm out of here! Now watch me work," I said.

I hit I-20 westward bound with big wheels blazing! I was headed home to Shreveport. Oh, my God! I was free at last, free at last. No mo' shackles, and I know I'm glad! I picked up the twins as soon as I got to town. Not only was it my freedom day but it was my mother's birthday, so I gifted her with a ticket to visit my sister in DC as my way of saying thanks for all she had so selflessly done for us. If she never did another thing in my life to help me, protecting my children from becoming wards of the state while keeping them all together was the blessing of a lifetime. And what better gift could I give to her than returning to resume my responsibilities?

Remington was in fourth grade by this time, and Lawrence was in first. I checked them both out of school and grabbed McDonald's hotcakes. We went to our favorite spot on the Shreveport riverfront and enjoyed our breakfast together under the midmorning sunshine. As was customary for us, we all rolled around on the grass and played tag until we were out of breath. The sun was certainly shining down bright on us.

It was such a glorious moment for me. Seeing those bright eyes and beautiful brown faces filled up all the places in my heart that felt empty and lost only the day before. In many ways, I know that Remington and Lawrence felt like they were getting their lives back. My return was like a breath of fresh air for them. They loved their mother. They loved the fun we've always had together. They remembered. Freedom and Justus, on the other hand, were struggling to warm up to me.

It broke my heart that the twins didn't know me. At least not in the way that their brothers did. They were only ten months old when I went to prison, and now they were three. The only mother they had ever known was their grandmother. Sadly, no memories of me existed. The part I appreciated most about my mother is that, although she filled my *place* she held my *space*. Whenever the twins would call her Mama, she would correct them and say, "I am not your mother. Sibil is your mother." I knew when I left for prison that this part would be challenging, but nothing could prepare me for that kind of disconnect.

Justus cried so much as a child. And Freedom was definitely Grandma's baby. In those first few days, I got a taste of the habits that they had formed in my absence. I got a chance to see the damage that Rob's and my actions had wrought on our innocent, defenseless children. Remington, the eldest, had been hit the hardest as he shouldered the bulk of the fallout. In our vibe sessions, Remi would bring me up to speed on the way my mother had been letting the twins get away with everything, and how he was happy I was home to get them straightened out.

It was a lot to take in. On the one hand, I was overjoyed to be home. But I was also anxious about all that laid ahead. Nevertheless, after those first twenty-four hours, I shifted my focus to getting the boys packed up for the morning road trip. The big day was upon us. In less than twenty-four hours, we would be Angola bound. I was determined to put my family *back together again*. Visiting their dad would be our family's reunion and the first step in reassuring the boys of this truth.

FOX AND ROB

When Fox was released, she was confronted with a whole different set of issues—raising children as a single parent, finding work as a formerly incarcerated person with felony charges, maintaining a relationship with a man serving sixty years behind bars. It was all so hard and painful. And yet, there was a thread of fortitude within her that kept the fire going in her heart.

Meanwhile, Rob had begun to establish himself as a mentor in prison. He'd earned the respect of the men and the staff. He was also beginning to be more and more intentional about his exit strategy.

For the both of us, we continued to dream. We continued to believe that something better was coming. We couldn't see it for sure. Everything around us told us not to get our hopes up. The prevailing question as always was, How do you dare to dream in the midst of hell?

Our answer? By faith.

"Now faith is the substance of things hoped for, the evidence of things not seen" (Heb. 11:1 KJV).

FOX

This would be the first time the twins had seen their father since they were babies, right before I left for prison. In fact, none of us had seen Rob since August 2000.

Now it was October 24, 2002, and the boys and I had gotten on the highway at two o'clock in the morning in order to make the five-hour drive to be at Angola when the gate opened at eight o'clock. About an hour into my trip, I stopped in Natchitoches to get coffee and gas. That's when the thought hit me, *Am I even on Rob's approved visiting list still?* Since I was newly released from prison and not sure of the policy regarding visitation with formerly incarcerated persons, I was concerned.

I was terribly exhausted when we arrived—but my visit was approved. I breathed in fully and said a quick prayer. *Thank you, Lord. Some sensibility has returned to my world.*

I got the kids. I got Rob. I got liberty. Now what? What will you have me do?

The boys were so happy. We sat down at the visitation table, and I felt such relief. It wasn't perfect. We were still behind prison walls. But for all practical purposes, this family was back together again. We could touch each other. I had the ability to make sure that my children knew their father.

As far as Rob and I were concerned, we were the epitome of what Rob always says: "If love were an acronym, it would be Life's Only Valid Expression." Our connection is powerful. Even in that dimly lit and sterile room, surrounded by cinder block walls, filled with the stench of years of cooked caramel corn, time stood still. It was just Rob, the boys, and me. The prison disappeared because our love overshadowed everything else around us. It was like we'd never missed a moment. The energy between us just ignited, and we fell right back into place with each other as if we'd never been apart. Looking into his eyes and holding his hand felt natural and safe, even in that space. It felt like home.

God's grace was ever-present during that first visit. After two days of visiting with Rob, we were preparing to go back home because I'd run out of money. That second day, I met a woman from Memphis, Tennessee, who was there visiting her husband. She informed me on how to get an extra visit. When you consider you only get two visits a month, the extra visit means so much. "I can actually visit again?!" I was so excited.

That would be great, I thought, *if I had the money to extend our stay at our hotel.*

She must have understood the look on my face because she said, "I've got two beds in my room. Me and my daughter can sleep in one, and you and the boys can sleep in the other, if you want."

I was so incredibly grateful. We needed that time. Being with Rob for the first time in so long, watching him with the boys, was healing to my wounded heart. It felt like I was on a high even if, in the back of my mind, I knew that the real world was out there waiting.

ROB

As for me, there was nothing greater than a thought whose time had come. Fox was home. In some ways, it seemed like the time had flown by. In other ways, it felt like it has stood still. Determined to maximize our time together, I had put in for a special visit. Like most prisons, Angola operates from a reward and punishment system in their efforts to manage the violence behind bars. Since I had been "good," I figured no one should bark at my request for an all-day outside park visit. I reminded the department head that I was write-up free, worked as an academic tutor and social mentor to others in the institution, and, most importantly, my wife and kids were traveling from afar.

The request was granted!

This is important to note because prison visits rarely last longer than two hours, and they usually happen in a covered shed. Instead, Fox, the boys, and I enjoyed our first homecoming visit outside under a brightly lit sky, on green pastures, and in a space equipped with a barbeque pit. Unfortunately, we could not take advantage of that particular accommodation because we couldn't afford the meat, charcoal, or lighter fluid.

During the visit, I noticed Remington looked like he could use some special attention. When they had first arrived, I took a mental note of the perplexed look on Remington's face. He wasn't quite himself. I could practically see his little brain working overtime trying to make sense of his family's new arrangement. I took him off to the side, away from everyone else. There he said, "Mom is home, but we still don't hear any talk of when you're going to come home, Dad."

Wow! I thought.

His heart was carrying way more emotionally than it should have been. But if I knew nothing else about my nine-year-old son, I knew that he was strong and wise beyond his years. And I knew that he trusted me. So I charged him as *man of the house*. On one hand, I felt this was robbing him of his childhood. But I also knew that if we were going to survive, we needed an all-hands-on-deck approach. I was reminded of how I felt whenever my father needed me to step up. Whenever he assigned me a title or put me in charge of a mission, things felt a lot less burdensome. I thought about the Jackson (as in the Jackson 5), Williams (as in Serena and Venus), and Kennedy (as in John F. and Robert) families, who raised exceptional children under what some might call tyranny and duress. As towering as the role was, Remi never disappointed.

I suppose the good thing was I didn't get the sense that he was resentful at all about any of it. I'm not sure he even knew to be. In fact, I think he was quite proud of the role and even felt a sense of purpose.

We joined the others back at the table, where we laughed, cried, and tossed the ball until our hearts were content. As the boys began to wind down after hours of play, Fox and I stole a moment to talk about the business and what next steps looked like. Weary, battered, and bruised, we both agreed that it would be a better conversation for the following day rather than the first day of our visit.

Overall, I tried my best that weekend to be in the moment, catching up and feeling all the love, joy, and happiness of being in that space together. For us, it was *our* family reunion. And none of us knew when we would see each other again. The challenge was balancing the other factors that were forever lurking over our heads. This journey was not over yet. Not by a long shot.

FOX AND ROB

The faith walk we were on was bigger than just believing our dreams could still come true or our marriage could withstand the test of time. It was more about whether our children, these little Black boys we loved so much, would survive and even thrive despite what their circumstances showed them. Could they escape the generational curses that can sometimes befall incarcerated families? Would our one tragic mistake and the extreme consequences we faced as a result seal their fate? The answer for us was always going to be an unequivocal *no*! So the work began. We needed Rob home—sooner rather than later.

ROB

The direct appeal timeline for my nephew Ontario and me went a little something like this: the original appeal was denied in November 2000, so by 2002, we were facing our last chance to challenge the court's sentencing directly.

My attorney and I had decided to illuminate the significant problems found in our original case hearing. Among other errors, I'd uncovered that one of the jurors in our case was a former client of the district attorney, and another juror had been a victim in a robbery, which could have certainly meant their partiality. We also submitted that our original confessions should have been suppressed because the state did not meet its burden of proving that the confessions were free and voluntary. There were so many threats of harsh sentencing and Fox's arrest that were thrown around in those first few days after the robbery. Finally, our defense attorney at the time had moved to have my case severed from my nephew's in light of the additional jury tampering charges I'd received. I knew that those charges could prevent him from getting a fair trial. The request for severance was denied though.

None of what we petitioned the court for in our appeal mattered. We were no match for a system that was designed and determined to keep us locked up for the maximum amount of time, regardless of whether the crime warranted it. And unfortunately, the court denied our original appeal again. The sentence was final. I'd been given what was called a *practical life sentence*. Even if I served only fifty of the sixty years, I would be almost eighty years old before I had an opportunity for release.

But the work for freedom didn't stop. It was now time for us to prepare to request post-conviction relief. This meant that we had to go back into the district court where I was initially sentenced and address more constitutional issues. In my research, I learned that I could petition for post-conviction relief on the basis of something called *ineffective assistance of counsel*. That seemed to be my strongest opportunity for leniency and relief. As a result, I filed a petition to the courts that my lawyer at the time, because of his lack of experience, had failed to file some much-needed motions in my case in order to preserve legal rights for me to entertain at a later date. It was a long shot, but I had to try. Not raising the issue was not an option.

As I read through the law and continued to research other cases, all I could see were the faces of my children—Remington, especially. I'd promised him that I was coming home, and I had no plans of letting him down.

FOX

After that first visit, I had to shift my focus. I didn't have anyone who could help me figure out this new life, so I needed to collect myself and stabilize our family. Remington was in a fantastic school in Shreveport, and, not wanting to uproot him again, I allowed him to stay there under the care of my mother until school was out. Meanwhile, Lawrence, the twins, and I stayed in Monroe where I had immediate access to resources to help me get us back on our feet.

Bright and early Monday morning, after our return from Angola, I awakened with hope in my heart. This was my first day back in my full-time role as a mother. I was back in the saddle. I got the fellows dressed and fed, and I tidied up our new place. My plan was to leave early because it would be Lawrence's first day at his new school and the twins' first day at their new daycare. I went out to warm up the car, and as Murphy's Law would have it, the car wouldn't start.

I'd been through so much in my life at that point, one would think that a broken-down car would be the least of the things that could get to me. But sometimes, it's the little triggers that unearth the pain we bury deep down inside of us. Sitting in that car, my heart finally broke. I cried my eyes out. Feelings of being lost and abandoned took over. I was so thankful the boys were still inside.

In hindsight, I realize that the reason I broke down at that moment was because I had kept moving from the time I'd pulled off from the halfway house, to our visit with Rob, to arriving in our new home. I'd never given myself even a minute to process what had happened. To sit with myself and say, "You are free."

After finally allowing myself to feel all the emotions that swelled in my body, I pulled myself together and started knocking on people's doors. It was seven o'clock in the morning, so I'm sure I annoyed some folks, but I needed to find someone who could give me a jump. I was fortunate to find someone willing to do it, only for it to not work at all. I needed a new battery. I found a ride to the auto store, picked up a battery, and got the car started. Finally, I got my boys off to school.

I can't deny that there was this ever-present reality check in the back of my mind that said, *Okay, Fox. You're home from prison. You're a convicted felon. How in the world are you going to make this work? Addressing Rob's sixty-one-year sentence while simultaneously spending the next three and a half years on parole yourself? What is this going to look like?* I can't necessarily say that it was the voice of doubt. If anything, it was my spirit making sure I was clear about what I needed to overcome. It outlined what my starting point truly looked like. I was holding back the fear.

Being in the halfway house for the latter part of my time served gave me some advantage. I was able to come home with money. I had access to resources that allowed me to secure a home in Monroe, find a school for Lawrence, and pick a daycare for the twins. The one-bedroom apartment we lived in was sparse, but it was ours. I'd found some decent furniture on the side of the road and bought a mattress that we put on the floor. It wasn't much, but it was enough for the four of us to begin our new life together.

"I miss you, Mama," Remington used to say whenever he called. "I want to be with you."

His words would cut me. I knew everyone was counting on me. I knew I couldn't fail.

When I came home from prison I wanted to launch my own TV show. It was something Rob and I had talked about in our letters and correspondence to each other while I was incarcerated. I felt strongly that if God was going to be gracious enough to allow me to get my freedom back, then I should use that freedom to do exactly what I felt called to do—speak to people. To share my testimony, yes, but also to give people insight on how to pursue their dreams no matter the odds. I wasn't entirely sure what would be required to do a TV show, but just like Paulo Coelho says in his powerful book *The Alchemist*, "When you want something, all the universe conspires in helping you to achieve it."[2]

To reflect on all this now is to really see just how the Spirit was working overtime in all our lives. I don't know how or why, but I was willing to dream, even while living in the midst of hell. There was no doubt in my mind that we were going to put our family back together again. I believed that we would get Rob out, simply because I was willing to die trying. Yet, I also had the immediate needs of my family to attend to. So, by the end of 2002, I realized that I needed to move back to Shreveport to make all these things happen. Remington's little voice rang loud in my heart: "I want to be with you."

I finished the semester and, in January 2003, moved into a studio apartment in downtown Shreveport with Remington, Lawrence, the twins, and now my cousin's son, who I'd taken in because my single parent male cousin needed support in raising him. Listen, when you have as many kids as I do, what difference does one more make?

In March, I launched *The Fox Rich Show*.

FOX AND ROB

Rob was making major headway within the incarcerated community in Angola as well as among those who might be able to help him outside of the prison. One such connection was NFL great Jim Brown, who Rob met as a graduate of the Amer-I-Can program. Brown founded the organization to address gang violence following the Rodney King riots. He impressed upon Rob that when making tough decisions one must "eliminate the negative, establish the facts, and then choose your best option."[3] Meanwhile, Fox was building a presence on television and in her community. If life had taught us nothing else, it's that the only place success comes before work is in the dictionary. There are never any shortcuts.

FOX

Of course, I wanted to do *The Fox Rich Show* to showcase my own talent. That was a given. But I also understood a fundamental principle about how the world works. Some people call it karma. The Bible says, "A man reaps what he sows" (Gal. 6:7). I knew that whatever I wanted for myself, I needed to do for others. Service would be my ticket to fulfilling my purpose. So I designed *The Fox Rich Show*'s format to be a talent showcase or variety show.

The idea came to me while I was in prison. There was a show that used to come on every Sunday morning called the *Earnie Miles Gospel Show*.[4] It was a gospel talent show on the local TV station in Monroe. Every Sunday morning, it was a big deal for us. Everyone in the dorm would gather around the only TV, twenty-six inches and wall-mounted, to see if somebody they knew was going to appear on the show and sing the house down. After watching several episodes, I wrote to Rob about the concept: "I've bought commercial time before for Culture so I'm wondering how much we'd have to pay for a full thirty-minute show?"

The urge started to take root and grow as I thought about how I could expand on the typical talent show concept and maybe even draw talent regionally and nationally. I saw the potential of shows like *American Idol* and *The Voice* before they aired.

It took a bit for Rob to catch on though. He gave me a

little pushback because he thought that when I was released I would reopen Culture and continue the journey we'd started. But during my time away, I came to the realization that God had a different calling for me. God was calling me to speak. And how do you speak to the masses? Television.

I'd already done a small, local show on the community channel before going to prison, so I'd already had a taste of what it would be like to be a TV show host. It was something I really wanted for myself, and I went into overdrive to make it happen.

First step? Find a location.

With the money Rob was able to line up for me from inside and my leftover student loan dollars, I ended up renting an old movie theater in the mall and converted it into Fox Rich Studios. It was a dusty place that hadn't been used for many years, but we went to work on it. We cleaned it from top to bottom and painted the walls. We removed the top and bottom cushions out of the three hundred theater seats and my sons, my nephew Adriel, and I spent days cleaning and painting each one with our own hands. From there, it was on! We signed a contract with the local Fox Network affiliate and *The Fox Rich Show* was ready to go live!

It was such an amazing time. In addition to hosting the show, I booked all the talent, secured the sponsors, and even cleaned the bathrooms before each show. I handled all the business. The buzz about it was growing, and people in my community were energized, if not all-out excited by what I was doing. In our first season on-air, we pulled in a three in the Nielsen ratings, beating out *The Steve Harvey Show* in our market. All I could think was, *Yes! This is what it means to walk in my purpose! Four months home from prison and I am literally on air! In more ways than one.*

ROB

"So, you say you wanna be a star?"

Despite all I was shouldering, I was excited! Fox was right where she wanted to be—onstage, in that little electric box called a TV, with a mic in her hand and everybody cheering, "It's *The Fox Rich Show*!" I'll be the first to admit that I had some reservations. I think at the onset, I was just trying to figure out what the game plan was going to be once Fox was home. We knew that we had to secure some of the basic necessities for her and the boys—a place to stay, transportation, and income. I think I just automatically thought she was going to fall back into doing Culture because there was still a void in the marketplace. I even figured that it would be an easier transition considering all we'd gleaned from the first iteration. But Culture was my dream, not hers, not anymore. And with each letter to me, it became clear what she wanted to do.

Ever since I've known Fox, she's been trying to get inside that little box. She has an anointed voice that galvanizes people and moves them into action when they hear it. She speaks to the heart. The television show would give her a wide audience to do exactly that. I wanted that for her. I truly believed that Fox could be the next great talk show host.

And to tell the truth, I couldn't stop her anyway. When Fox has a certain level of conviction about something, there is no stopping her. Even as a voice of reason, I have to concede.

When she's ready to fly, my role is to help her get the rocket fueled, hook up the jets, and make it go fast. And even from prison, I was determined to do exactly that.

About this same time, I started working as a mentor with PREP in prison. PREP is an acronym for Pre-Release Exit Program. It was usually for people who were serving sentences of seven years or less. People in this program were housed in a separate area of the penitentiary and were tutored by guys who were serving much lengthier sentences. The hope was that these men would be a positive influence on the PREP participants and help them return home more equipped to manage their lives' affairs.

There were so many young brothers I got a chance to speak life into during that program, but one gentleman in particular was a young brother from New Orleans. He really amplified the impact I was making as well as helped me refine the skills I would need later on to help my own case. This brother was fighting a serious conviction, and I was able to help him create a strategy for dealing with the open charge. I shared with him how I believed retroactivity could apply in his case. He ultimately ended up taking a deal and was sentenced to ten years.

After that experience, he and I became thick as thieves. We worked out together, broke bread together, and dreamed together. At his core, he was a man with integrity and became my family.

In one encounter, I shared with him Fox's idea for the variety television show. "Man," he said, "I have a bit of money on the outside. I want to invest in what you and Fox are doing."

His words took me totally by surprise. Not that he was interested, but that he even had access to that kind of money.

I would later learn he had been enriched from a personal injury lawsuit settlement.

Fox had found her lane, and by God, I'd found her a funder.

My friend offered us the seed capital to jump-start *The Fox Rich Show*, and everything took off from there. Like I said, rocket fuel!

Soon after, his mom came to visit to discuss the particulars. Later that day, he turned to me and said, "You know this is the first time my mother has ever visited me, bro?"

I was taken aback. To think, this was the first time this man's mother visited him during his entire ten-year sentence. It was heart-wrenching to consider. She'd chosen to do so because I'd spoken with her a couple of nights before over the telephone and shared with her the progress her son was making and a little about the opportunity he was trying to be a part of. Like most serving time, he had his own family traumas that remained unhealed. But I will never forget the words his mother said to me before leaving the visiting area.

"The man who sits here . . . my son . . . is not the same man who came to prison. Thank you."

What a transformative moment! I was literally seeing God working all things for our good in real time. It was humbling to know that I was able to play a small part in helping this family find their way back to one another.

It was a crazed opening night. I called Fox as she was going onstage. I could hear the roaring noises and commotion in the audience. *The Fox Rich Show* was now *live*! Although I couldn't be there, my heart beat wild with anticipation. The thought of her fulfilling a dream was absolutely exhilarating.

FOX

That night was a big deal in town! The house was packed. I remember hitting that stage and taking my cell phone with me. I wanted Rob to hear and be a part of what he'd helped to make happen. I made the introductions, and we were off. Folks went crazy about all the entertainment I had lined up. The energy was through the roof! This was a win not only for us but for our city!

ROB

It wasn't just that I was rooting for Fox, though I absolutely was. I was also rooting for myself. For our family. Imagine being in the lowest moment of your life. You've essentially been condemned to hell by a system that was never interested in seeing you as a whole human being in the first place, that is intent on breaking you down and making you feel less than. It starts with something as simple as assigning you a number. Assigning you the label of *inmate*. Making you do hard labor to earn pennies. I think, subconsciously, I was always trying to find ways to acknowledge my humanity to myself and those around me. To counter it all. Some days it was something as simple as giving another incarcerated man a bag of chips that I'd gotten from the commissary because they were starving in the middle of the night and didn't have money on their books.

So being able to create seed capital for my wife's vision while inside the bowels of prison, to give her the opportunity to do something she loved doing, was beyond rewarding. After all, ain't I a man?

FOX

The Fox Rich Show had two amazing seasons. I was so proud of the work we did expanding the show into the Lake Charles and Monroe markets. But because it was paid programming, I needed to have the resources to be able to sustain that kind of expansion. Unfortunately, airtime was incredibly expensive, and I didn't have enough financial support to generate the ad sales in order to maintain the show. It became so hard to keep the show going while raising the boys and still working with Rob on his case.

The general manager of the CBS affiliate in Shreveport saw how big the show was in the community and offered me a deal to pick up the show. Sadly, that deal included them keeping all the money made from the sale of commercial ads—the very place I made the little bit of money I had to support our family. It was definitely a huge opportunity but just wasn't a good deal for our circumstances, and I had to bow out. When it got to the point when I had to choose between paying for airtime and buying the kids some shoes from Payless, something had to give.

I made the difficult decision to end the show.

Winston Churchill once said, "Success always demands a greater effort."[5] *The Fox Rich Show* ultimately failed, but that was okay. I would build the next thing. That's what I do. That's what we do. So I shifted gears. In the spring of 2004, I launched the Power Party College Tour. Without a second thought, I packed our boys into the car and hit the road, where I spoke candidly to college students all across the country on a plethora of topics—from the prison industrial complex to the power of family to the dynamics of male-female relationships. I soon became known as "the realist speaker of the twenty-first century" by HBCU college students across the nation. The more I empowered others, the more empowered I became.

FOX AND ROB

There was no settling. Not for Rob, inside working desperately to get free. And not for Fox, determined to be a voice for the voiceless. We still heard the voices of people who didn't believe in us. We knew that our reputations were shot. But we also knew that our success was not just the best revenge but the best testimony to God's redemptive nature. The best way we knew how to get back at a system that was never about rehabilitation and only intent on obliterating families was for both of us to succeed in life and business.

Even now, having both been slaves in America's system of mass incarceration, we have a sincere appreciation for what it means to be truly free—in mind, body, and spirit. To be free means that you are living out your life on your own terms with agency. Even back then, when sometimes the walls felt like they were caving in or we struggled to make ends meet, we refused to devalue what we knew about freedom. Pursuing our dreams, at that point, became less of a selfish ambition and more about walking in God's purpose for our lives. To do anything less would have been dishonorable to Fox's newfound freedom and the freedom that Rob was working so hard to attain. And with that freedom would come the ultimate family reunion.

7

MC MEANS
MOVE THE CROWD

When you have a dream, you got to grab it and never let go.

Carol Burnett

FOX

When I ended the show, my brain kicked into over-drive. I thought, *What's next? What can I do with little to no money?* Too often we get so busy looking outside ourselves when everything we need is already in us.

I still wanted to host a television show. It was a way for me to reach more people at one time. But I thought that if I couldn't do television immediately, nothing could stop me from talking to people. It didn't matter if I was standing on a street corner, I could capture an audience. Marcus Garvey used to stand on a soapbox and preach his message of Black economic empowerment. My passion was always speaking. It is my gift. And my voice was something that didn't require any inventory, purchases, or ad sales in order to be profitable.

What about a power party?

The concept was downloaded into my spirit and made so much sense to me. That's what I'd been doing all along. For myself. For the women in the prison. For the people in my community. I was empowering them, teaching them the necessity of resilience. I decided that I was going to use my voice to remind everyone who'd listen just how powerful God had made them. How no setback in their lives had the final say. I mean, my life was a literal testimony of that very thing, right?

In January 2004, I sat down and wrote a plan for what a power party speaking tour would look like. Since March was Women's History Month, why not make my first audience women? I had grown so much as a woman, wife, mother, and daughter, so it felt right to pass some of what I'd learned on. As women, we are the womb of all mankind. I knew that if these women could recognize their power, they would be able to stare down anything that tried to steal it from them and succeed anyhow.

A good friend and mentor of mine Roxanne Johnson was the executive director of the Shreveport YWCA during this time. She was one of the first people to support Culture years prior. I gave her my vision for the power party and explained how I wanted to go on tour speaking to women.

"Well, you can make your first stop at the YWCA. Let me know when you want to do it," she said.

I was so happy. She was once again supporting a dream of mine, and my heart overflowed with gratitude.

"Wow! Thank you! You know, what better day to talk about the power of women than on the day of love?" I asked.

She agreed. My very first power party was held on February 14, 2004, at the YWCA in Shreveport, Louisiana. Believe it or not, we had a rare snowfall that day. At first, I was worried that people wouldn't show up, but I was wrong. These women needed this as much as I did. The turnout was amazing.

I stood on that stage with a mic in my hand, dressed in a beautiful white evening gown I'd found in a local thrift shop, and spoke from my heart. I wanted the women to leave that space knowing that they had the power to change their lives. To build upon what was good and transform any pain, hardship, or mistake into something useful.

In the middle of my speech, I started a chant that the women and I recited over and over throughout the night.

"I've got the power! The power is in me!"

"I've got the power! The power is in me!"

"I've got the power! The power is in me!"

I was in my element. That mantra was not only something I gave those women but also an affirmation of my own strength. From there, the Power Party Tour was off and running. I leveraged that one speaking engagement to secure other dates and began tapping my network of friends and acquaintances in the area. A friend who worked at Wiley College brought me to campus to speak to the women there, which gained me entry to a number of historically Black colleges and universities. I expanded my content to include men and did some men's events to speak to their specific challenges. I understood very early on the influence of romantic relationships and wanted to see how my words could inspire unity between Black men and women for the betterment of our community. Who better to talk about such a thing? Rob and I were taking on the whole State of Louisiana for our life, liberty, and our freedom. I knew that we were stronger together than we could ever be apart.

One of my favorite topics to speak on was the dynamics of the Black family and the family as a core institution. One year at Medgar Evers College in New York, I spoke candidly on what I'd learned about the power of the family which, in hindsight, aligns with where my heart and mind were all along.

> That mentality of Black men not being able to do right has a rippling effect on the Black household. Family is first about the power and strength in numbers. When you can find someone to walk this life with you, there is a richness and wealth in that, Great Ones, which far supersedes anything we can print. Like money.

I spent that entire summer of 2004 booking out the tour for the fall. In September, my first stop was Mississippi Valley State University. I rented a van, put my boys in homeschool so they could travel with me, and began this next phase of the dream.

After I got my first check from speaking, I bought a little Mazda stick shift from a guy on our street—which promptly broke down not too long afterward. Finally, my mom helped me buy a reliable ride, and the boys and I hit the highway. I spoke everywhere from Florida A&M University in Tallahassee to Medgar Evers College in New York City. Traveling that far north also gave me the chance to connect with our son Mahlik's mother in New Jersey. It was important for the three of us as parents to make sure the boys spent time getting to know their brother, so she allowed Mahlik to join us for a week on our tour up the East Coast.

That was truly a blessing.

My boys were learning as much as I did on the road, including being exposed to Black men and women scholars who were serious about their education. Early on the speaking tour, we'd gone to South Carolina State University, and many students came up to me asking about the boys.

"Oh, these are your kids?"

"Yes, they're all my sons."

I can only imagine the positive impression that was made on students who might have also been parents. But one thing I did notice is that my boys didn't know how to formally introduce themselves or anyone else. The twins were five, Lawrence was eight, and Remington was eleven. As someone who spoke for a living, this was unacceptable. So, part of what I embedded in their homeschool curriculum was how to speak and give a proper introduction. They became my team; everyone was a part of the show. They started introducing me at all of my engagements. Their little voices would be strong and powerful as they introduced the crowd to their beloved mama. The audience ate it up! Remi was the hype man. He warmed up the crowd. Freedom and Justus were the greeters and helped Big Law (Lawrence) with the back-of-house sales. And when Remi wasn't introducing me, he was the cameraman.

Anytime a child can stand up on a stage in front of a crowd

of people, sometimes thousands of students, and introduce their mama, it gives them a competitive edge. It was not much different from what my mother did for us when she signed us up to speak at every program our church held—Easter, Christmas, MLK Day, Pastor's anniversary, you name it. There is no doubt in my mind that this experience of being on the road served the boys well as they went back to school and later to college. Taking that particular leap of faith feels like the greatest investment I made in them.

I continued our spring tour because I was in great demand and doing exceptionally well as a speaker. I got off the road and started flying in and out for engagements while the boys briefly returned to public school full-time with my mother acting as their caretaker.

FOX AND ROB

Another major reason why the Power Party College Tour was so important for Fox was because Black students needed to know that Black people cannot afford to commit a crime in America; they will pay far more than they will ever gain. The system is not going to treat them fairly or impartially.

We wanted them to know that the best thing they could do is never find themselves in the system, never break the law. We were college-educated people and still found ourselves as slaves in this country, thanks to the exception clause found in the Constitution's thirteenth amendment. It was a hard truth, but one we needed them to understand. One must not check themselves in to slavery.

As hard as we strived to make a life for ourselves, in and out of prison, it was less about the grind and more about having faith that our lives could be more than what society or even our own bad decisions said they had to be. One of the significant parts of the Power Party College Tour was when Fox would have the boys put mustard seeds in little envelopes and hand them to the students. It was not just a message to them that said, "When you're feeling down, when you're feeling challenged, take out this mustard seed and see just how little faith it takes for you to move forward in the direction of your dreams." It was a symbol of how we were pressing through the troubled season of our lives. Like Jesus said, faith the size of a mustard seed is all we need to move our mountains (see Matt. 17:20).

8

HEAVY IS THE HEAD THAT WEARS THE CROWN

Our crown has already been bought and paid for. All we have to do is wear it.

> Toni Morrison's review of James Baldwin

FOX AND ROB

The faith journey we were on as we navigated being an incarcerated family was very much individualized at this time. Rob had his path to walk, and Fox had hers. Nearly eight years into this experience, we knew that we both needed to find out what God was saying to us personally in order to figure out our next steps as a family unit. For Rob, that meant exploring a number of faith traditions and ultimately attending Bible College. For Fox, it meant unlearning some of the things she was taught about the roles she had as a wife and mother. The church that we both were familiar with tended to see the role of women in the church in very narrow terms. But Fox was a part of a new generation of spiritual thinkers with a more holistic approach. She was in pain, and she knew if she did not take care of herself, she could not take care of anyone else. And although we were both deeply committed to a philosophy of unity within the institution of marriage and had clear ideals on what it meant to be a good parent, we also understood that we had to give consideration to our own wellness. If we did not tend to our individual walk with God, then nothing else mattered. Rob could not be a good husband and father, and Fox would not be able to be a good wife and mother if we didn't carve a clear spiritual path for ourselves and our own healing as individuals.

ROB

By the time my conviction had become final, I was the lead facilitator for PREP and began to see the work I was doing with the young men in the program as an offering to and from God. I saw it as my opportunity to serve.

Usually, inside of any prison, there's some hallmark program that exists as a way to bring positive press to the facility. There's been so much conversation about the lack of actual rehabilitation within the prison industrial complex that these programs are designed to somehow counter those narratives (though they never seem to consider the way the system of incarceration itself—as opposed to any individual program—perpetuates recidivism). Around 2005, Angola had two such programs. PREP, as I explained, was designed to help men with shorter sentences reintegrate into mainstream society. The other program was the prison's Bible College. The New Orleans Baptist Theological Seminary program was a new entry into the prison that received its funding through faith-based initiative grants under the Bush administration.

I took advantage of everything available to me as a lead facilitator with PREP. Because I was a tutor and mentor, I got access to everything the guys who were in the program had access to. I slept in the same dormitory with them, and any and all educational programs that they had, I did too. One of the most pivotal moments I had working in the program was attending a job fair that was designed to help the men line up opportunities post-release. While there, I started having a conversation with a woman who thought I might be an asset to her program.

"How much time do you have left?"

She was shocked when I answered that I had a sixty-one-year sentence.

Sixty-one years is a practical life sentence. For many, that's hard to process.

"Oh my God, baby! How do you wake up and do this every day?"

I paused and pondered while looking her over. She carried herself so well. She looked like someone I was supposed to speak to when I walked in the room.

"This outfit you have on," I said, breaking the silence. "Did you pick it out this morning, last night, or what?"

Confused, she answered, "I had it figured out last night. I knew I was coming up here this morning."

"Well, I guess, in the same way you picked out the outfit, never once considering whether or not you would live to see the next day, I pick out how I'm going to move through my time inside of prison. But, like you, I've witnessed enough yesterdays to know that tomorrow will come. So I, too, dress and move accordingly."

A light sparked in the woman's eyes. I could tell she wouldn't soon forget that conversation.

As a prerequisite to acceptance into the highly sought-after Bible College program, I was required to attend a seminar series based on Henry Blackaby's book *Experiencing God*.[1] It was a one-year program that led to a certificate that would be our entry into the college itself. The coursework in that program changed the trajectory of my spiritual life. There was one course titled Making Peace with Your Past that helped me see that there was truly a pathway to redemption. I also got a chance to truly unpack the whole concept of faith. This belief in something we do not have evidence of and cannot see. I learned to identify all the things that we, as human beings, put our faith in, even beyond our understanding of God and Jesus, Allah and Muhammad.

Those courses were such a clarifying agent for my spirit. Because once I was able to grasp that redemption was possible for me, I could justify my hope in an earlier release—even in the face of a system that wanted to keep me bound. And once I was really able to dig into what faith was and what it looked like, I knew that the one thing I trusted was also true: God was going to deliver me. I believed it with every fiber of my being. And no, I didn't have evidence to support this. I didn't know how it was going to happen or unfold. But I knew salvation was real. I certainly didn't think it would take twenty years. But I did believe that I would hold my boys and wife again without chains or shackles. I had witnessed other people with life sentences go home before me, so that meant it was possible. After all, nothing is impossible with God.

It was inside those moments of learning that my faith began to grow and develop. I was exposed to so many faith traditions while in Angola. I was initially drawn to the Muslims because they tended to be part of many of the same educational programs. The tenets of their faith, especially for Black Muslims, focused on seeking knowledge, so education was a huge priority. I was also a seeker of knowledge, spending much time in the law library and reading, so they seemed to gravitate toward me in general, sometimes in the hopes of converting me.

I already had an affinity for Islam as a way of life. I was partly influenced as a follower and lover of hip-hop; many of the early artists like Public Enemy, A Tribe Called Quest, and Boogie Down Productions identified with some variation or sect of Islam. Its presence and rhetoric were definitely woven into the music, and for many years, I felt like something almost Muslim. The language of the religion became infused into my life.

Interestingly enough, I felt very much the same about Christianity in the beginning. I knew guys who attended the Bible studies and church services in prison and were dedicated to their life as saved and sanctified.

I suppose I struggled to grasp one particular religion even when faced with these doctrines that were attracting my attention. Some of that has to do with the fact that my mother and father were not hyper-religious people. I understood

God. A higher power. The Creator. And I was drawn to these manifestations of faith and spirituality, but I wasn't yet sure about the details. I saw myself as the bee in a story I heard a Muslim friend tell. The bee travels from one flower to the next, taking exactly what it needs from each flower in order to make honey. It doesn't discriminate. It doesn't necessarily care whether the flower is a dandelion or made of seersucker. It's merely trying to gain some pollen to do what's necessary to make its sweetness. Much in the same way, at this stage of my life, I was simply looking for truth.

I learned that prayer could show up in a myriad of ways, but it always seemed to rely on consistency. I watched how having obligatory prayers throughout the day allowed the people around me to be pulled into a moment of stillness where they couldn't help but sense the very presence of God. Muslims pray five times a day. Buddhists often choose the morning for meditation and reflection. Christians, while stating that we should pray without ceasing, also tend to use the morning or evening as a time of communion. I was fascinated by the idea that people all around the world were submitting their petitions to God at the same time.

My ritual was to get up early in the morning, and when we were allowed outside, I'd sit on what we called the ledge. This was during breakfast, when everyone else was in the cafeteria eating, which provided me a rare moment of quiet time—and I came to crave the quiet even more than a morning meal. The ledge was a stone lip that sat just outside the dormitory and mimicked a balcony if we were living in an apartment. The overhang made for perfect seating, and if I made it out in time, I could catch the sunrise in the morning and the sunset in the evening. What made it even more of a powerful experience was, as I sat on the ledge, the call would go out for the morning or evening prayer of Islam, and there would be this indescribable peace that would come over me.

Whenever I sat on the ledge, I sat on the end over the boot wash. The boot wash was a concrete spot where guys coming in from the field would use a faucet to wash all the mud, dirt, and debris off their boots before walking inside the dormitory. Now, in the morning, there would be no one using the boot wash yet; so, to add to the peaceful surroundings, I'd turn on the water in order to capture the tranquil sound of water falling. It was the closest thing I could get to a waterfall. Even in the evenings, when I'd return to the ledge to watch the sunset, I'd sit in the lotus position with the water falling as the sun would recede into the night.

I can't say that I was reciting any particular prayer in these moments. I was mostly trying to be still and centered in the moment. It was usually a time for me to ease my mind from all of what was tormenting me. It was a kind of internal spiritual clemency from the pain and emotional upheaval that quaked inside my soul. In that sacred time, while in the midst of the heartache and terrors of being bound, of watching a man get stabbed in the dormitory, or of another man who overdosed, I could unwind and release. It was my version of letting go and letting God. A man I'd met along my path once told me to let go of my ego because ego was nothing more than an acronym that meant Easing God Out. One of my professors in college would say, "Look, you've got to get over yourself. This ain't about you. This is about the kingdom." Sitting on that ledge in the morning and evening was my way of easing God back in. It was my way of orienting myself toward God's will for my life.

Yes, I desired to be home. I desired to be anywhere but prison. But in words often attributed to Buddha, you have to "be where you are . . . otherwise you will miss most of your life."[2] God had assigned me to this lot in life for an unknown period of time. I was being called to walk the walk of faith.

When I entered Bible College around 2009, after a pit stop in a yearlong graphic design program, I started realizing even more that Christians had deep truths in their text, some of which even aligned with what Muslims adhered to. So I began to walk that path to see if my own faith walk could be strengthened by what I was learning. And as I did, God met me where I was. I kept coming into these small victories—one being that I had three hundred men under my tutelage over the course of my six years as a leader in PREP—that I hoped would lead to a really big victory.

God used my time in the program to give me a platform. The state of Louisiana at that time had a recidivism rate of 62 percent. That meant if one hundred people go home, sixty-two of them would come back within three to five years. For the guys who'd gone through PREP at Angola under my leadership, the recidivism rate was less than 5 percent.

The prison staff wanted to know what I was doing. "How is this even possible?" they'd ask.

By the time the next job fair rolled around, my name was in the mouths of a number of people. I ended up meeting the same woman I'd met the year before, only this time, I knew exactly who she was. Her name was Sharon Weston Broome, and she was there gaining support for her bid for a state representative seat. She would ultimately serve two terms and become a senator of our state, and at this writing, she is Mayor of Baton Rouge, Louisiana—the first African

American woman to ever hold the seat. She became a wonderful friend to me in my fight for freedom.

FOX AND ROB

While Rob's faith journey seemed to always lead him back to the hope of release, Fox's journey focused on staying free—in mind and spirit. She was focused on parenting our children in such a way that they wouldn't make the same mistakes we did, but she also made sure they could draw upon the strength and fortitude that was their birthright. This is the journey of incarcerated families. Two parents on very different paths that hopefully will lead back to a wholeness they are forever seeking.

FOX

I had to be a double parent. When my children needed something, when they had a question, there was no other option but for me to answer that need or question. There was no "Go ask your father," or "What did your dad say about that?" I recognized very early on that I couldn't do this by myself. If it was my duty to raise them to be young men, I needed to teach them everything that I was doing to survive, maybe even earlier than most kids would need to know it.

I'm reminded of our ancestors who grew their own food. They couldn't afford for their children to lay around. The kids were required to contribute to the household. Well, in my household, our family's livelihood, our economy, rested in whatever entrepreneurial venture we had going on at the moment. Whether it was *The Fox Rich Show* or the Power

Party College Tour, everyone did their part, because this is how we ate.

I can honestly say that this was the primary area where my faith was stretched. I was in a position where I had to trust that God would turn those extra hands and tummies I loved from what some people might call weights into assets. And that wasn't always easy. I choose not to believe that anything about the way my children were raised was something that God couldn't and didn't work out for their highest good. Yes, they were fed and clothed. I did what I had to in order to ensure that. But even above basic provisions, my children were nurtured and loved. They were taught survival and resilience. And those things are the most quintessential offerings we can give our children.

My faith walk was fueled by my determination to care for and love my babies. In the midst of every storm, I chose to deal in truth. The truth of my circumstances. The truth of theirs. The truth of their father's. I did not lie to them. I did not cover up the hard places. I believed Scripture when it says you "shall know the truth, and the truth shall make you free" (John 8:32 KJV). No matter what our lives looked like, I wanted my boys to understand that liberation was the goal.

I think I started praying more around the time I was released. When I had to start tackling what life would be like for me and the boys. I also started meditating more. I would go down to the riverfront in the morning and watch the sunrise. I had to wrestle my fear. I had to reckon with being scared because I knew that everybody around me was depending on me. I also knew that I did not have the answers. Yet failure was not an option. Breaking the law again was not an option. I had to figure out this new life with no map.

No model. No training. And I knew God was the only one who could show me the way.

I had to tune in to the Holy Spirit and allow myself to be led. I made many decisions based on the sense that something didn't feel right. I relied on hearing from God for every single movement and action. I had to, really. It became like breathing. Faith became like oxygen to me—I couldn't see it, but it was always there. I never knew what the next step was. I couldn't see what was going to happen on this journey. I just had to breathe and put one foot in front of the other and trust that the next step would be divinely ordered.

FOX AND ROB

The experience of incarcerated families is a unique one. In many cases, it's women who are left waiting. Wives, girlfriends, mothers, grandmothers, aunts, and caregivers. They find themselves laying away much of the time, waiting to reunite with their family members, waiting to put their families back together again. One of the most important things women on this journey must remember, though, is that they are the ones who are free. And they must live as free as they possibly can—in mind, body, and spirit—until their person comes home. That's not easy to do. In fact, sometimes it's only by the grace of God that they are able to hold on themselves. Even though their partners are incarcerated, they can only own the part they played.

It wasn't Fox's fault that Rob was sentenced to sixty years. She'd done her time. She'd done what the state required of her. She couldn't live in guilt because she was home and he was not. The next phase of her journey was about taking care of the family while continuing to support our legal agenda—an agenda that would include the uncovering of the misinterpretation of a law that could set Rob free. But God was also revealing to her that she could not put her whole life on hold while waiting for Rob to return home. Especially since tomorrow isn't promised. As Rob was working and, in his own way, praying, Fox was also centering herself. And both of us, in the midst of our wait, were being restored.

9

I TOLD THE STORM

He calmed the storm to a whisper
and stilled the waves.

Psalm 107:29 (NLT)

ROB

Even though *The Fox Rich Show* was shut down, I still loved the concept and thought it would be great to start something like it within the prison. I pitched the idea of a variety show or talent showcase to the warden as a way to restore offender morale. Violence in the prison was at an all-time high—like something they'd never witnessed before—and I suggested that something like this might help.

If I had to live there, then I wanted the space to have as much peace as possible. That meant taking a more proactive role as a member of this community. I chose to call the prison a "gated community" to shift and change how the residents saw themselves. Gratefully, the guys started to buy into it also. "Well that puts a new spin on things," they'd say. And it did. I wasn't ignoring reality; how could I? We were faced with the reality of our situation every day. But dignifying the language of how we spoke about the place and how we spoke about each other created a little bit of light in a space that felt perpetually dark.

I also started a program that I named DevelopMental Movement. It was in an effort to *develop* the *mental* state of the guys serving time alongside me—including expanding their educational options, since a vast majority of them had less than a fourth-grade education. I'd seen firsthand the destruction and violence that can occur when uneducated people who are angry to the point of rage and are frustrated with themselves and the system that has shown them no care are put in close quarters. Every day in prison is a day in a war zone. We were in conflict with either the security guards, the men who lived next door to us, the men we were bunking with, or the men we ran into some mornings in the showers. It was turbulent all the time. Someone was always getting hit over the head or scalded with hot water or coffee. It wasn't uncommon to wake up in the middle of the night to screams and yells. The trauma was constant. It was like living in a war zone. People were always trying to numb the pain, so they'd do whatever drugs they could get their hands on. Security guards were underpaid, so they were more likely than not to bring us whatever it was we requested and pocket the profit. Prepaid cell phones were a hot commodity and ran us about $500 despite the guard only paying ten bucks for them at Walmart. Guns, knives, drugs—there was always a guard willing to get it for you.

The only way I knew how to counter being constantly in-undated with violence was with the very thing I'd somehow been able to hold on to throughout my entire experience—love. The bedrock of what I've always believed was that love is *Life's Only Valid Expression*. And love was the only force strong enough to subdue chaos when *Living Inside Violent Energy*. I needed to pour love on these men, and on myself, in order for any of us to survive.

The Develop*Mental* Movement addressed violence in the prison by using music and the arts as a salve. I was reminded of my studies from long ago about how the enslaved would communicate to each other using spirituals and songs. They'd share coded information about opportunities to escape or plans for uprising. Plantation owners and overseers never really thought anything of these songs. They just thought it was a bunch of dark workers in the field trying to make light of a bad situation. But there was power in that music. Not just as a way to communicate but as a way to take ownership of themselves, to have some agency over their lives. It brought about healing in the face of constant violence.

I went around the prison looking for the most popular spoken-word poets, including my nephew Ontario, and the program's first event was a weekly poetry night. I recruited a few guys to help me put it together, and we invited guys to the poetry event during call out, the time set aside for us to go to evening educational programs. On our night, I would occupy a classroom space and charge guys a pack of cigarettes to come sit in. In addition to the show, they'd get a full meal that I was able to negotiate with some guys who worked in the kitchen. I'd get a box of raw chicken—one hundred pieces—from them for about eighteen dollars and break it down into two-piece meals with fries and bread. I stored my food from week to week in the freezers at other clubs I had access to and worked out a deal with the security guards to let me come in the kitchen and cook everything.

You couldn't beat it. The men could come and eat well and enjoy some powerful words from these poets who could have easily graced the national stage in another life. They loved it because, for a moment, they didn't feel like they were in prison. It felt like they were in a country club. I'd like to think the ambiance and vibe in there was its own kind of healing balm.

Even the guards were catching the vibe and enjoying the weekly escape. And not just the male guards either. In 2002, Angola had begun to allow women guards and staff to serve in close quarters with the men who were in prison. Most of them were recruited from high school because they were not planning to go to college. The pay was very low, and many of the male guards had quit, so the prison replaced them with women in order to get away with paying low wages. The problem with this was that many of the women were first responders when dealing with the violence and conflict. I could tell by their faces that many were afraid. I can only imagine what it was like when the lights went out at the end of the day, being a female staff member locked in the dormitory with one hundred men.

As a result, many of them sought protection from us. They knew that if something went down, it would take too long for a male security officer to run from the captain's office all the way down the walk that was about five hundred yards away.

So as part of building my program, I started providing protection for the women guards in exchange for things we needed. Not drugs or phones or guns. I wanted programming.

Dr. Michael Eric Dyson had put together a program around his book *Holler If You Hear Me: Searching for Tupac Shakur*, which included a screening of a documentary about Shakur. In exchange for protection and peace of mind, the female guards and staff allowed me to use the large space for a call out in order to host the screening and conversation. I charged guys to attend the screening, and to my surprise, nearly three hundred men showed up.

So now, in addition to serving my brothers through the Develop*Mental* Movement, helping to keep the sisters who worked with us safe, and doing my part to boost the morale in the prison, I was able to make money for myself and my family. It was a win-win-win.

FOX

Let me tell you something. *This* is what I love about this man. He firmly believes that it ain't what you got; it's what you do with what you got. We'd done so much for so long with so little, we were truly experts at making something out of nothing. He created a movement within those prison walls, and I know there are men who owe not just their lives but their very sanity to Rob's ingenuity.

ROB

And I wasn't done. Not by a long shot. I created another program based on a book I was reading about a chess guru who'd go to prisons and play against inmates in a chess tournament. He would play up to eight guys at one time, and sometimes, one of the players would give him a good run.

I came up with this sixteen-week chess tournament that would eliminate people from week to week until it culminated in a New Year's Eve championship game. Of course, I would charge the guys to participate, offering a one-time prize for the winner based on the amount of money made. I also charged the audience for attending, which gave me the opportunity to stack my account. I was, as rapper KRS One said, delivering edutainment—education through entertainment—to the masses.[1]

I was utilizing the algorithms of chess in an effort to turn the tumblers of each player's and each observer's mind. I taught them that the way a person might make decisions about their moves in a chess game—sometimes seeing six or seven moves up the board—was the same way a person could make decisions about their life. I had conversations with the men about short-term and long-term goals. We talked about how to compartmentalize those things, even as it related to their convictions, in order to work through an achievement or exit plan.

It was always about making sure everybody won.

FOX

Not only that, watch how God turned this man's work into an opportunity to bless him.

ROB

Yes, exactly. The championship game of the chess tournament was creating a huge buzz around Angola. It ended up being a battle between a Black man and a white man, unfortunately splitting the prison along racial lines. Even the wardens had gotten involved—sometimes coming to watch on their days off—because the white guy was a hobby craft specialist who had a good relationship with the administration.

On the day of the championship, there were about three hundred guys in the building watching the chess tournament. With the help of my staff sisters, I was able to hire a DJ to come spin records and have TV screens playing music videos posted throughout the space. Again, the setting mattered. The men didn't feel like they were in a prison. They were able to breathe, if only for a few hours.

After the tournament ended, word got out about all that I was doing. There were people high-up who celebrated my work, so I knew that it was time for me to shift gears a bit and focus on my case again. My post-conviction relief request still lingered, but I'd begun to set my eyes on the possibility of a pardon.

On January 14, 2005, Senator Charles Jones from Monroe, Louisiana, came to speak to us as part of the prison's Martin Luther King Day programming. I was determined to speak to him about my case. However, it was a challenge to get close to him because the guards had roped off the area where he and other distinguished guests were seated.

I was able to get a few of the guys who I'd hired for security at the events to catch Senator Jones as he was leaving the podium and block off the section where he and his team were headed. Then they made room for me to speak with the woman who'd escorted him into the space. I told her that he used to be my lawyer and if nothing else, I'd like to have a word with him.

"Well, yeah. For you, Rob, of course."

Thank God for favor.

"You know there will be a bunch of people trying to get at him, so make it fast," she quipped.

She didn't know that I already had my contingency plan in place for that. My security guys were going to make sure that no one got in front of me to speak to him. When I finally got to the senator, it was smooth sailing.

"Hey, Robert! You know your wife has been calling me? Man, I wish I had a wife half as good as yours."

FOX

I bet he did.

ROB

At that time, Kathleen Blanco—our first woman governor in Louisiana—had been elected to office a few years back, partly because of Senator Jones's influence. In our conversation, Jones shared that he had the governor's ear, which made me think he could possibly get my matter in front of her in hopes that she would sign my commutation of sentence.

Jones was a well sought after attorney-turned-senator who selected his clients carefully. He was good at his job, and his representation would come at a price.

"How much?" I asked.

He leaned in and whispered so that only I could hear: "I don't know if it's going to cost you a little or a lot, but I need you to know it's going to cost you." Of course, he wasn't going to give me a number right then and there. What lawyer worth their salt would do that before reviewing the details of the case?

So I heard him loud and clear and adjusted my expectations accordingly. We had a lot of fundraising ahead of us.

"I'm going to just give you my number. Have your family come see me. We'll have that discussion then," he continued. "Because my money ain't going to come out of this prison. It's good seeing you again. Take care of yourself."

And just like that, he went back into politician mode. The visit was over.

I couldn't wait to get back to my dormitory and write or call Fox. We were almost there.

FOX

$25,000.

That was how much it was going to cost us to hire Jones to represent Robert on a pardon. And Jones felt strongly that with the mounting injustice and Rob's relationships, we would be successful in petitioning the governor for relief. But I'm not going to lie, I was frustrated. It always came back to money. We'd blown so much money over the years with a myriad of attorneys, from Kidd to Jones, alleging that they could get us through this process and failing every single time. The truth is, we didn't have $25,000. And Rob's oldest sister, whose son Ontario was locked up with him, was mostly tapped out also.

Beyond just attorney fees, the system makes it so hard for anyone to appeal their case beyond conviction. The transcripts from the previous court proceedings alone, needed for our matter to even be heard and our injustices addressed, cost $8,000.

This system wanted Rob to do his time. Which might have been understandable if the sentence matched the crime. But because it didn't, and we had precedent after precedent showing that it didn't, we continued to fight. I was going to knock on every door and turn over every leaf. Or at least I was until August 28, 2005.

FOX AND ROB

On August 28, 2005, Hurricane Katrina breached the levees in New Orleans and terrorized the Gulf states of Louisiana, Alabama, and Mississippi. Electricity, gas, and food were scarce. Angola prison sat in a blackout. There was no power. No way to call family members to see if everyone was okay. The prisoners were given frightening messages of what was happening by the staff. Everything was underwater. People were standing on the roofs of their homes, waiting, hoping to be saved. It was like the ocean had become the land, and we all were simply trying to stay afloat. For us, that was true in more ways than one.

FOX

Right before Katrina hit, I'd been ready to go out on my fall speaking tour. Everything was planned. I was going to start at the bottom of the Louisiana "boot" and work my way up. I was so confident that I would not only impact every audience I stood in front of, but I could make enough money to take care of the boys and me and raise the funds we needed for Senator Jones to represent Rob in the pardon process. My very first gig was at Xavier University, a historically Black university right in New Orleans whose campus was so severely damaged by the storm that the entire fall semester was canceled. The following gig was at Southern University in Baton Rouge, another campus beat up by Katrina. Needless to say, both engagements were canceled.

It was like Katrina had taken the wind out of us just when we'd begun to fly.

Desperate to put my fall tour back together, I started booking out of state. The boys and I headed out to Bowie University and the University of Maryland, Eastern Shore. Heading to the East Coast felt right. And since the boys were with me, I was also able to take them to DC for the ten-year anniversary of the Million Man March, which happened to be held on the twins' birthday, October 16.

I made a whole day and night out of it. We camped out on the National Mall, and it was hilarious to see the boys all laid out on blankets, thinking it was the most epic sleepover ever. But I also let them know that the moment was so much bigger than just a fun trip with Mom. We were there to commemorate an incredible occasion when more than a million Black men descended on DC to commit to the economics and social preservation of their families and communities, to challenge the prevailing narratives and extend each other grace and resources for the road ahead.

It was an absolutely beautiful day out there. Only two months out from the devastation of Hurricane Katrina my family was together—even if Rob was on the phone—for such a momentous event. I felt so empowered. Like God was smiling down on us despite whatever we'd gone through.

ROB

Of course, I called Fox at the scheduled time so I could catch them while they were out there. Just the thought of my boys in that space where I once stood just ten years prior flooded me with emotion. I felt so good. Like in the midst of all my mistakes and miscalculations, we'd done something right. That moment also gave me hope. Hope that we'd return to some kind of normalcy after the hurricane shook everything up.

I also got a chance to talk to the brothers in my dormitory about the march and all it inspired, which led to my stock continuing to rise among the men and the staff. As I talked more about the social ills that the march addressed, I began adding in things I'd learned from my readings. I'd read *The Spirit of a Man* by Iyanla Vanzant, *Man's Search for Meaning* by Victor Frankl, *A Prisoner's Wife* by Asha Bandele, *Long Walk to Freedom* by Nelson Mandela, and a number of books by Michael Eric Dyson, bell hooks, and countless others. People were not only seeing Fox and me as people they could trust but we were beginning to see how God was positioning us as social justice leaders. We just hoped that we could keep that momentum going.

We were not impacted by Katrina materially, but we knew so many people who did lose everything. Their properties were just washed down the river, and they were left asking God what was next for them. Our hearts were broken.

We were, however, impacted by Katrina in other ways. So much of our legal strategy was contingent on the state recovering from its devastation—the same state that had just ushered in a Republican governor in the form of Bobby

Jindal, who basically ran on a platform that said he was not signing any pardons. Just like the long history of prison life in Louisiana denotes, governors (some former wardens) have always operated much like the plantation owners of yester-year. With just the stroke of their pen, they were able to grant liberty or death.

It felt like someone had stabbed us in our hearts. No one knows what freedom means until they've been a slave. And we don't have to be locked behind prison walls to be a prisoner. In this life, there are many things, people, and situations that keep us locked up. And the systems that surround us don't help.

The prison population grew from 5,000 to around 6,300 due to prison shutdowns. Jindal's budget cuts also meant programs were stopped. Milk was rationed out once a week. Real fruit was taken off the menu and only given to people who had dietary restrictions of some kind. Desserts were cut, except on Sunday when they served cinnamon rolls. Now most of our meals consisted of red beans and rice and tuna fish instead of fried fish on Fridays. Morale was beyond low. Between all the changes that I was experiencing as a result of the changes brought on by Louisiana's new administration, and Fox still struggling to make ends meet, we both held on tight to our mustard seeds.

As a result of all these changes and shifting priorities, I started spending more time in the law library, learning about state laws, examining and reexamining my case. I truly felt like I was getting close to going home, despite the new governor. But I also knew that Fox needed more than just this verbal reassurance.

10

A SOUL COMES FORTH

Pleasure gets lost under the weight of oppression, and it is
liberatory work to reclaim it.

Adrienne Maree Brown, *Pleasure Activism*

FOX

People have always commented on the physical chemistry that's present between us. There's an energy that seems to ignite whenever we are together. Even in those years when we were apart or in other relationships, it didn't take much time for either of us to long for that spark again. We know we are very much like kindling to each other. So when Rob was sentenced to sixty years in prison, we were confronted with a very real challenge above and beyond the legal one, above and beyond the real needs of our family. Louisiana leads the world in incarceration per capita but has yet to consider practices that reinforce family ties. There are other states that allow conjugal visits as a correctional treatment strategy, but not the Pelican state. When you are incarcerated, you not only lose your freedom but you lose your humanity as well. The lack of physical intimacy was taking a serious toll on both of us. We found ourselves wondering what breaking the law had to do with our very real sexual needs as human beings and particularly as a married couple. We were forced to grieve the loss of intimacy. The loss of touch.

One time, we were sitting in the visiting room of Angola talking and longing for each other. It was such a tender moment. Rob started rubbing my forearm, and I was savoring even that small, seemingly benign touch from him. Suddenly, the security guard came over to our table, and I thought, *Oh Lord, what in the world does she want?*

"I'm going to need you to stop touching her arm like that," she said.

Rob and I just stared at each other. *What in the . . . ?*

"Where's that in the policy?" Rob protested.

Her face was stoic and unyielding. "You heard me. I'm going to need you to stop touching her arm like that."

I honestly think that the intimacy Rob was showing in that moment, combined with the natural fire that swirls around us anyway, made the guard uneasy.

It was like being separated from each other wasn't enough. The dehumanization had to extend to a deprivation of intimacy. It's the clearest demonstration of how prison is solely designed for punishment and not rehabilitation. If the latter was a priority, then this kind of intimacy and care would be encouraged, not banished. The healing balm that tenderness and physical touch can offer even the hardest of men should have been championed.

ROB

I can only compare it to what many studies have already shown about what happens to babies when they go without the touch of their loved ones. The impact and effects are often devastating. When it comes to babies, we call *that* neglect and trauma. But I don't believe the results of these studies only apply to children. Prison was a great place for me to observe what happens when grown people are required to go without a certain amount of love, intimacy, or any other physical expression of care by those who love us. Some of the men serving time had not been touched by a loved one in decades, and they were hardened. I always wondered how, if there was no room or tolerance for compassion and intimacy for these men, the system expected them to somehow fully rehabilitate into caring and law-abiding citizens. I mean, some did. By the grace of God, they were able to hold on to that part of themselves. But it seemed counterintuitive, to say the least. Of course, I now know that the system could not care less about the rehabilitation of these men. It was only concerned with enforcing these inhumane and archaic rules that would constantly remind us of our unworthiness.

When a person comes to visit a loved one in prison, they are only allowed two kisses and two hugs. One when they arrive, and one when they leave. That is about the extent of direct contact one can have. But something as simple as me rubbing Fox's arm wasn't usually an action we were checked on. Most guards didn't say anything. That's why it was startling when this one did.

Nevertheless, Fox and I were always going to find a way to not only express our intimacy with one another but to tend the fire that God had put between us. Touching became a signature of our visits. Her forearm. My fingers. Her waist. My bicep.

FOX

Just how determined were we? Well, let's just say I let Rob talk me into an unexpected conjugal experience during one of the prison's rare and special events. I'll never forget it.

ROB

I talked *you* into it?

Okay, so maybe I did.

But I don't recall you complaining.

FOX

I didn't complain but I was floored when Rob told me, "I got us twenty minutes together this Saturday."

"You're lying, right?"

Listen, all I knew was that I had been celibate for six and a half years. It had been over half a decade since I'd gotten the chance to touch him like that.

When Saturday came, there were competing emotions happening in my body. I was excited. It felt like we were teenagers sneaking away from our parents to be together.

But we weren't teenagers. My excitement gave way to fear. I was terrified.

Oh, Lord, have mercy.

As nervous as I was, I just kept coming back to six and a half years. I had to try.

ROB

We did more than try.

But admittedly, it was a bit nerve-racking, even for me.

FOX

We had twenty minutes to be together but only used two of them. When we touched, it was over as quickly as it had begun.

ROB

I mean, it had been a long time.

FOX

We had no idea just how significant that day would be. Not just because our rendezvous gave us an opportunity to be together as husband and wife in a way that we had not been able to in a very long time. But that day, we reclaimed our freedom. We had a moment of liberating pleasure.

It felt like dumb luck. I couldn't even remember when my last period was because, after being celibate for so long, I'd long stopped keeping up with it in the same way I did before.

It wasn't until I was back home that I realized our rendezvous occurred right smack in the middle of my cycle. Prime ovulation time. But even then, I didn't think that this one isolated time would mean I'd be pregnant. I joked around about it, but *what were the odds?*

Apparently, the odds were in my favor.

When my period didn't come, I went to Family Dollar and got a pregnancy test. I couldn't bring myself to wait until I got home, so right there, in a disheveled dollar store bathroom, I took the test.

When I saw the result, I laughed out loud.

Then I cried.

Then I laughed and cried again.

Admittedly, I'd been in worse situations. Like when I found out about the twins while in handcuffs and shackles. But still, I couldn't help but think, *I need another kid like I need a hole in my head*. It was unbelievable.

"Fox, you know you don't have to do it. You know you don't have to have it," Rob said.

Wait, what?

I was taken aback. Abortion was not an option for me. In hindsight, I understand that Rob was simply trying to make sure we weighed out *all* our options. I had not yet learned it was okay to weigh out *all* my options, no matter how difficult the options were to consider. I'd been there before. The very first time I had sexual intercourse at fifteen, I ended up pregnant and had an abortion. I wasn't unfamiliar with the process or all that comes with it. But I was grown now. And as much as things looked bleak in terms of our finances, I believed in the power and blessing of the life that was growing inside me.

I mean, after six and a half years of celibacy, Rob barely touches me and this soul comes forth? For this life to come through these extreme and restricted conditions, I knew he or she was obviously something special. Rob and I were going to have to gird up and figure this out. That moment was bigger than us or our circumstances. My mind was whirling, but at the time, I just told him, "I will go to the clinic, just to see."

A new law had passed that required an ultrasound before a person could get an abortion. I prayed hard during the days leading up to that visit. *God, I will see this through. I will have my baby, but just don't let it be two.* I knew I couldn't handle another set of twins on my own. It wasn't possible. I barely had resources for another single child. *Please, God.*

My prayers were heard. There was only one soul in my womb.

"Okay, we are going to figure it out," I said to Rob.

And yes, I knew that the bulk of care was going to fall on me. I had four children at home. Growing boys who needed so much from me already. And a growing but still unsteady income. I knew that it would be hard in light of everything I had going on at the time, everything I was trying to build. But I strongly felt that the life inside me was bigger than anything I was going through.

ROB

I'm not sure I was pushing Fox toward an abortion as much as I was offering her the space and opportunity to weigh all of her options. I should have been more emotionally supportive, but I couldn't be in that moment. Being in prison, it was always safer for me to think about things analytically, logically, and that carried over in this case. The facts were what they were. I knew Fox would ultimately be responsible for everything, and the last thing I wanted was for her to, once again, navigate the pregnancy and birth without me there. She'd been through too much. At this same time, I was learning so much about decision-making in a class I had been taking that I think my response may have come out more stonehearted than I intended.

In Jim Brown's Amer-I-Can program at Angola that I'd just completed, we were taught that whenever you find yourself in a critical decision-making process, there's a specific way to make the decision. First, I had to eliminate the negative. I had to establish the facts, and choose my best option from there. So that's what I did when she told me she was pregnant. I looked at all the facts. I was in jail serving a practical life sentence. She was caring for four other children and trying to build a business. Our money was stretched and limited. And we still had a long legal battle ahead of us. Those were the facts, and I wanted Fox to consider them. Unfortunately, all that intellectual processing of information doesn't always include the sensitivity and empathy we should have when dealing with other humans. It doesn't account for the leaps of faith that God might be calling us to make in any particular moment.

FOX

Another *fact* that I had to consider was that, at this time, we had just experienced the most momentum in Rob's case we'd ever had before. The pastor of the church I'd recently joined, Little Union Baptist Church, had given me a voice in the community again. I was teaching Sunday school, and when we weren't on the road traveling, I had both a space and venue to speak what God had placed on my heart. Just that summer, my pastor had set up a meeting with the president of the bank we'd robbed, and I was able to go there and make amends on Rob's and my own behalf. The pastor also knew the district attorney who had prosecuted us and was willing to go and talk to him for us.

ROB

It was a sincere act, for sure. We genuinely cared about the hurt and trauma we caused the tellers that day, and we'd known for some time we needed to do what we could to make things right in a community where we had done such wrong. On the legal side of things, making amends was also a recommendation from Charles Jones. He said that we would have a hard time convincing the courts of anything if we didn't address the victims. That made sense and aligned with where our hearts were.

Unfortunately, there was no support to be had from the district attorney, Bob Levy. In essence, he'd sent me to Angola to die, and that seemed to be what he intended for me to do.

FOX

Then we lost the support of Senator Charles Jones because the entire attention of the state of Louisiana remained on recovery and restoration in the aftermath of Hurricane Katrina. Any connection we might have at the state level was no longer valid because of the circumstances. So there we were, preparing for the holidays and a new year with Rob's case dead in the water and me pregnant. I had a couple of checks coming from previous speaking engagements, but after that, everything would come to a screeching halt.

Even my children were concerned. Remington, maybe even thinking about how much more I would need his help, said, "Mama, you don't have to do this."

I had to laugh to keep from crying. Everything felt hopeless.

ROB

That year was, by far, one of the hardest Christmases we had in the whole twenty years we were incarcerated.

FOX AND ROB

Through it all, we kept going. The turn of the new year saw Fox doing whatever she could to bring awareness to what was happening in the prison industrial complex as well as serve our community. She coordinated a voter registration drive featuring Erykah Badu at Southern University in Baton Rouge and continued creating events when she could.

Rob had begun to dive into his classes in seminary as well as unpacking the 20/45 geriatric parole law. Could this be the thing that potentially leads to his and many others' exodus from prison? We didn't know. But we were going to keep trying.

It was an extremely rough pregnancy for Fox, who'd spent a big portion of it terribly sick. Not to mention that she'd begun to feel more and more isolated and afraid about the uncertain future that lay ahead. The lack of stability was weighing on her more than ever. But glory was coming. Or a version of it anyway. Robert Fox Richardson II, or Little Robert, was born August 11, 2006, and we were headed toward the most unexpected shift in the history of our entire relationship.

11

WHAT YOU WON'T DO FOR LOVE

It's not the load that breaks you down,
it's the way you carry it.

Lena Horne

ROB

I t's only been in recent years that there has been any public discourse around the ways trauma of any kind can affect our lives. For Black folks, conversations about post-traumatic slave syndrome—a concept coined by scholar Joy DeGruy that links the multigenerational trauma of racial injustice and violence to the way our communities exist today[1]—and the work of Dr. Bessel van der Kolk, author of *The Body Keeps the Score*—a book that unpacks the

174

way stress and trauma show up in the body[2]—have slowly unveiled the source of the mental and physical health challenges that are particular to our experience. But in 2007, while imprisoned in Angola, those revelations were still a long way off.

The things I saw while imprisoned in Angola will forever be etched in my mind. It will always be something I will wrestle with as I, even to this day, continue to unravel myself from the trauma of my experience. But the unintended consequence of that nonstop trauma and my unrelenting focus on my own legal issues was that it negatively impacted my marriage.

I was coming up on twelve years in prison, and I wanted out. There were other men who'd gotten less time for more heinous crimes. I wanted to be with Fox and my boys. Around this same time, there was a man Lamont Mathews who was president of the Lifers organization in Angola. He was also mentoring me. One day, he came up to me, and the urgency in his eyes was palpable.

"Did you see the latest advances in legislation as it relates to your charge?"

Wait, what?

As he continued to explain, I was bewildered. I had only really been focusing on my case from a litigation standpoint. It never occurred to me how a change in legislation might impact my case. The Lifers organization in the prison does exactly that though. Constantly searching for liberty, they comb recent legislation regularly to find opportunities for those serving life sentences. So Lamont was far more steeped in knowledge when it came to this.

"There is a new lawmaker out of New Iberia, Louisiana,

Phil Haney, a former district attorney, who has been working to eradicate geriatric parole," Lamont said.

Among people who were doing time, geriatric parole was called 20/45 or the Old Timers Law. This law allowed for all non–life serving offenders who had served twenty years or more in prison and were at least forty-five years old to seek parole.

I couldn't believe what I was hearing because I was sentenced to sixty-one years *without* the possibility of parole. But now he was telling me the law had changed in my favor?

Lamont opened up a book and read the highlighted passage to me:

> Notwithstanding any other law to the contrary and as provided for, in subsection A(2) of this paragraph, any person who has been sentenced to a term or terms of years for more than 30 years and reached the age of 45 and have served at least 20 years in prison, is eligible for parole consideration.[3]

It was like foreign language to me. But ultimately, I would turn those words over and over in my mind.

"What am I supposed to do with this?" I asked.

"Wrestle with it," he said. "It'll come to you."

Haney had been seeking a new interpretation of the law, particularly as it related to armed robbers. He'd gone through the attorney general's office for a revision of the law as he believed armed robbers were excluded from this particular parole possibility. The state considered his position, but the Department of Corrections took the findings of Haney and wrote it in their policy books, despite it not having yet passed at the state level. The law was reinterpreted to say that anyone who was in prison from January 1, 1997, forward for crimes of armed robbery was no longer eligible for 20/45 release. Unfortunately, I was arrested September 16, 1997.

My purpose was unlocked at that moment. Not only was I going to work to fight any future reinterpretation of the law but I was going to use it to gain my freedom. They were not going to steal my parachute from me and leave me free-falling in that hellhole.

What I felt in that moment could not be called hope. It was a recognition that I had been called. Called to fight for my freedom and the freedom of others. I considered it my purpose in suffering.

Haney was trying to wipe away the very thing that could bring me home to my people, to my family. Add that to the low morale and high violence within the prison, the loss of funding, changes in menu, and an additional 1,300 prisoners including women being transitioned into our already tight facility all because of the new governor. Some days, it felt like the walls were closing in. It felt impossible. But I'd read Matthew 19:26 where Jesus looked at the people around him and said, "Humanly speaking, it is impossible. But with God everything is possible" (NLT). So, I kept pushing forward, knowing that God *is* and *was* possible.

How does one hold all that pain? I do not know. Even today, it's hard to articulate the impact of the torment that lodged itself deep in my body and soul as I watched people die in that place. Not just physically die, although that was common too, but mentally and spiritually die slow, agonizing deaths. It was a living death. I didn't want that for them or myself. I don't believe that you can cage a man the way our system has done and expect full and total recovery. Even if one rehabilitates their actions, something is lost behind those bars in those cinder block cells. Something that only God can return. Something I pray for daily.

My faith walk was tested, but I was determined to continue wrestling with the language of 20/45, which restored some of my hope and vigor. I turned my attention to understanding the dynamics of how we'd gotten to a point where the Department of Corrections had chosen to reinterpret the law in their books, despite the fact that Haney's efforts had ultimately failed.

In 2006, when the state tried to pass the revision, it got out of committee but was killed before it ever got to the floor for further discussion, much less a vote. I knew that in accordance with the Louisiana Administrative Procedure Act, the Department of Corrections secretary had the power to alter rules and regulations necessary for the administration and function of the department. But there were exceptions. One such exception is when the exercise of power resulted in a "manifestly erroneous interpretation of law."[4] Why the department secretary chose to promulgate an erroneous rule that overlooked a well-established law was quite puzzling. Regardless, I refused to be denied.

The only thing standing in the way of my freedom was a technicality, a blatant misinterpretation of a law.

FOX AND ROB

This felt like good news to us. Or at least the potential for good news. Rob had stumbled upon something that could not only cut his time by two-thirds but ultimately free a whole lot of others. But his deep dive into legislation, the way it consumed him, meant that he wasn't paying attention to what was happening in his relationships. And then, the unthinkable happened. Rob's father passed away.

FOX

I remember holding little Robert in my arms. I was dressed in an all-white two-piece suit for Rob's dad's funeral. I had used my relationships with a few lawmakers to make sure that Rob could attend, despite all the upheaval and resistance from the current state administration. Because he was a model prisoner, one of our state senators called the Department of Corrections and requested his presence. Rob was transported to Shreveport for the funeral. When he finally arrived, I could tell something had changed in him. His eyes were different—like a light had been turned off. I saw the coldest version of him I had ever witnessed. He wasn't tender anymore. The attention he always gave, the desire to make me feel safe no matter our circumstances, was gone. My words of encouragement fell on deaf ears.

I had no idea what he was dealing with in Angola. He didn't talk much about all the ways the prison had changed under the new administration. He just shut down. And it was at that moment, I knew that I had to shift my focus. I had to attend to what I actually had control over.

I had five children—six including Mahlik, who still visited with us once a year—and no time frame for when their father was going to return home. I had very little money. Katrina and then my pregnancy had put a hold on the speaking engagements and other opportunities. I was depressed and anxious most of the time. Everything was resting in my lap, and I was falling apart.

How did I get in this space?

After twelve years, I thought for sure that somebody would've seen that we were not these horrible people who deserved life in prison. That somebody, anybody we'd talked to over that space and time would've been able to give us the answers as to how to rectify this wrong. But we were still waiting, still fighting.

One day that spring, I was at the house and realized that I didn't have enough money to pay the rent and the collegiate semester was coming to a close. I had one last gig booked at North Carolina Agricultural and Technical State University, and after that, I knew that future checks from speaking on the college circuit would not happen until the fall. I was in a financial crisis and needed to make a humbling decision.

I moved back home to my mother's house.

It was not something I wanted to do ever again, but I also knew that I could pay bills there and possibly catch up, catch my breath. But I wasn't going to let the temporary arrangement steal my dreams from me. I made a commitment to my sons—Remington in particular, because he was my biggest champion in the family—that while yes, we were going to have to move back in with Mama, we were moving back so that I could save and buy us a house. Yes, it was going to be a little inconvenient. A little tight. And yes, Mama could be a lot to deal with, but if we could survive it, if they would give me one year, I was going to get us a house.

I was at the lowest point of my life so far. I was trying to figure out the next step and applying for food stamps and anything else I could to tide us over in the meantime. That was one of the few times I ever had to elicit social services on this journey, but I wasn't going to let my pride get in the way. In fact, in true go-getter fashion, I found a way to make it work. When you get food stamps, you use them to purchase groceries. But the amount of groceries I was able to buy for five children was way more than we ate. So I took some of the leftovers and made lunch plates that I took down to the local car dealership to sell for money and pay the note on our van so we'd continue to have transportation.

By September, I was actively looking for a job because, although it was the fall semester, no one was booking me for new speaking engagements. I was desperate once again. No money to put gas in our van. No money to put on Rob's books or even communicate via collect phone calls. There was an ever-growing distance between Rob and me that was tearing my heart apart.

It had gotten bad. When I went to visit Rob, he didn't hold my hand anymore. He'd give me a peck of a kiss that he might as well have kept for all the emotion it expressed. I was hurting and not used to this at all. For the first time in nearly twenty years, the fire between us had gone out.

Later, sitting in my mama's house with a baby and four other rambunctious boys, I completely broke down.

God, give me the answer. What is it?

I stood up and looked at myself in the mirror.

I don't understand. I'm trying to live right. I'm trying to do the right thing. What is it that I need to know? Help me understand it. Make it plain for me.

I was pleading with God.

"Well, what do you want, Fox? You want a divorce?"

Rob's words struck me like I'd been hit by lightning. As low as I was, divorce had never crossed my mind. I just wanted to talk about what was happening. I'd pulled together enough money so he could call home, and I think I was hoping for reassurance that we were going to be alright. I needed him to know how my heart was breaking and that the load had become too heavy to carry. I wanted his help. We were Fox and Rob. We had never used the word *divorce* before. Where was that coming from?

He'd planted a seed.

I wanted Rob to know that I loved him. Oh, how I loved my husband. But everything it meant to have a husband, I didn't have. Did love mean that I had to sacrifice myself? My children? I was never going to give up on him. On the day of his sentence, I committed to never let go of his hand. But how could I keep my word and find the relief I so desperately needed? Because of the stress, my hair was falling out and my teeth were crumbling in my mouth. I was literally falling apart.

ROB

One of the most inhumane side effects of prolonged suffering is losing your mind. I was grieving the loss of my father, angry about the deplorable living conditions of the prison, and the thought of Fox's inevitable departure was strangling the life out of me. I was struggling to hold on. *How long can I sustain the idea of us being together as long as we are apart like this?*

I was confiding in an Asian friend of mine one day, and he

explained that in his culture, when faced with similar marital situations, the man would let the woman go. He said that they would never let their wives go through what Fox had gone through. In his framing of things, such a letting go was an act of kindness.

But I didn't want a divorce. I never wanted a divorce. And if I'm honest, I never thought she'd actually go through with it.

Later that evening, a calm came over me as I contemplated my friend's words. I steeled myself against the emotional tidal wave by doing what I'd done before—letting myself go numb. I emotionally checked out.

FOX

The seed of this word, spoken in our marriage for the very first time, took root in my heart. At first, it grew into a question. Then, as it was watered by fear and loss of hope, the question grew into the most painful decision I had ever made.

I called my cousin, who was a paralegal at the time.

"I need a divorce."

I don't even remember how I told Rob. I just remember the trigger. The first time he mentioned divorce, I'd immediately put it out of the question. That wasn't an option for me. For us. But when times got desolate, he made the offhanded suggestion that I bring some marijuana on my next visit so he could use it to make us some money, and that pissed me off. Yes, we were broke as hell, but by no means could we consider breaking the law! It was the straw that broke the camel's back.

"Are you serious?! With all we got at stake?"

I had no understanding of the desperation he was feeling on his side. All I could see was the desperation on mine. I'd sold lunch plates at car dealerships, and I can't even cook. I was combing the ads for jobs that might, maybe, possibly hire a convicted felon.

And yet, even as I had the divorce paperwork drawn up in November 2007, I still could not file it. It was more than the request for marijuana though. It was a culmination of everything. It would take me a year to follow through on it though.

ROB

That blindsided me, for sure. I knew that she loved me, and I think that, despite my callous ways, she recognized that I loved her as well. So when it didn't happen in the coming days, weeks, months after mentioning divorce, I didn't think that she would do it. After a year, it felt like it was coming out of nowhere.

In that season of this experience, my mantra was, "Just get out of prison. Get out of prison. Get out of prison." I wanted to get out at all costs. But the cost had become greater than I'd ever imagined when it affected my marriage. I was sinking in my own desperation and had been thinking that something different had to happen. Whatever that difference was, it had to be something that required me to only rely on myself in order to pull through. I knew I'd established goodwill with my fellow prisoners and the prison staff, so I wanted to try to create an economy for myself, especially since we were increasingly being required to pay for medical co-pays and other things that were once provided. I couldn't rely on anybody else. Not even Fox. I needed to stay focused on what was most important—getting out.

FOX

I saw an ad for a salesperson at a Cadillac car dealership in the newspaper, and since I'd sold them some lunches, I went back up there and asked them for the job. I knew they hired people who had been formerly incarcerated because I knew a couple of their employees. I also knew that if someone with my background could get employed in this space, I could make a decent salary. They hired me on the spot, contingent upon me not selling any more lunches—they hated my cooking.

I felt like my life had been saved. Not only did I go to work that Monday, but I sold a car on my first day! After that, I got really bold. I asked for an advance on my paycheck. I needed $1,000 because my car was about to be repossessed, and I needed it to get to work.

By the grace of God, they believed in me. By the end of the month, I'd put eight cars on the books and was salesperson of the month.

And guess what? That house I promised my babies? I was *so* close to buying it.

My mother had raised me in a home, yet Rob and I lost our home when we went to prison. That left my children growing up never knowing a home of their own. I was tired of them being bumped from apartment to apartment, and while I was grateful for my mother's little house on Easy Street, the neighborhood had changed since I was three and my mother purchased the house. When I left for college, the crack epidemic fueled by an uncompassionate system took over. We now lived up the street from the projects. Our community was brimming with violence. They'd started shooting in the neighborhood, and there were many days that I had to tell the boys to get on the floor because we didn't know where the damn bullets were coming from.

I wasn't going to allow my children to live like that all because of some bad decisions their daddy and I had made. They were going to have and do better. Just two months after being at the car dealership, I put together a plan for getting a house. Between my salary and a few speaking engagements here and there, along with my mom's income and credit, we had what we needed to buy a house. Mama and I could split the house note on the new house and rent out the house on Easy Street for additional income. We found this beautiful five-bedroom home with two primary ensuites and were on our way.

It wasn't just about moving and getting a house though. Between the hours I was working at the dealership, the travel I was doing for speaking—which was starting to pick up, and the effort I was making to raise these children properly, two adults needed to be in the house. My mother was the other adult available to me at the time. I knew she would provide for and protect my boys. My children were going to have a two-parent household, no matter what those parents looked like. And, with Ms. Peggy's help, we made it work.

I'll never forget sharing all this with Rob during a visit. I was so excited. Even though I'd begun the divorce proceedings, I still wore my wedding ring. I was still connected to him. His response?

"I need a lawyer."

Rob wanted me to take the money I had been saving for

a house and once again invest in legal representation. He believed that everything we made needed to be invested in getting him out. But this time, my answer was no. I was going to use this cash to buy these children a house. We were going to get out of the hood that he didn't have to see or live in. He didn't have to see the bus ride my babies had to take to school. At some point, they had to come first. I wanted better for our children, so no, I couldn't get him an attorney. I took the money and bought us a house.

ROB

I don't think I understood it that way. There was a huge part of me that was simply focused on what I was learning about the 20/45 law. I wish I could have seen it more holistically, but I couldn't at the time. I'm not sure I thought anything was wrong. I didn't think what we had was unrecoverable.

After talking to other prison wives, Fox asked why we didn't go to banquets. Banquets were special functions authorized by the warden of the institution. Approved girlfriends and wives of men serving time were allowed to reenter the prison following visitation to visit privately. In my efforts to stoke the dimming flame between us, I started to sign up for them and bring Fox in as often as possible. The ice on my heart started to thaw.

In hindsight though, I think there was a part of me that was angry about talks of a divorce. I wanted her to understand why I couldn't feel things in the same ways she could. I had to go numb; otherwise, those emotions would swallow me whole. I was not going to be able to survive if I let myself feel the fullness of my anguish.

In my mind, we didn't have to actually divorce. We could have just separated. Divorce felt so final.

FOX

We were at an impasse. Rob was trying to get me to understand this new information about the 20/45 law so I could better represent him when speaking to people on his behalf. He wanted to spend our visitation time studying the law together and brainstorming ideas like we'd always done. But I was no longer willing to use the limited time I had to spend with him in that way. I didn't have the capacity to learn anything else because I was so starved for the emotional security and spiritual connection we once had. I still wore my wedding ring, despite the pending divorce, because I wasn't ready to let go. I felt like, if we didn't make it, the system won. The system of mass incarceration was designed to enslave, yes, but also to tear families apart.

We just couldn't understand each other. So even though neither of us wanted it, on August 28, 2008, our divorce was final.

12

MOTHER OF INVENTION

Keep planting and sowing, living and knowing: beautiful
things take time, and that is okay.

Morgan Harper Nichols, Instagram post

FOX AND ROB

The one thing that we learned throughout this entire journey is just how much God is in the process.
Over and over, we've been able to use the things,
scenarios, and systems that made us feel the most harm and
turn them into fuel to move forward. Trusting God's hand
in the process of reinvention and redemption has been an
ever-present necessity for us. In the year before and after the
finalization of our divorce, Fox had shut down somewhat. It
was as if letting go was necessary for her to address her own

mental health. Letting go also helped Rob be able to shift all his focus to his legal case and to tend to his own heart and mind. There were still some bumps in the road ahead. We just had to decide whether those hurdles would finally take us out or catapult us back into each other's arms. A radical love knows no obstacle.

FOX

Meanwhile, I'd had the dream of writing a book within me for some time. *I've got everything I need in order to write this book*, I thought. It was my story. My observations. My heart. All on the page. Well, the digital page, at least. And I hoped selling it would generate some additional income.

In the heat of a Louisiana summer, I sat with a folding chair out on the blacktop lot of the car dealership, exposed to the blazing sun so I didn't miss any customers. With my new cell phone's Word app, I wrote out my entire book with two thumbs. Sixty days later, I typed "The End." Thirty days later, on October 9, 2009, I'd self-published and released *The One That Got Away*.[1] Having been spared the practical life sentence that Rob and Ontario received, I realized, much like the fox who escapes the vicious trap of hunters, I was blessed to be the one who got away. But I now had a personal responsibility to use my voice to warn others. I had to bear witness to what these laws were doing to my people and my community as someone who was deeply impacted by it.

There were a few reasons why I wanted to write my story. First and foremost, I wanted to bear witness to what I'd observed in the prison system ever since I started my prison sentence in 2000. When I got into the women's facility, I saw firsthand what was happening, what the experiences were, and I couldn't help but be devastated. *How can they treat people like this?* Often, the drinking water was green. Seventy-five women were packed into overcrowded, smoke-filled dormitories, imprisoned and forced to pay medical co-payments even though we were only paid 0.02 cents an hour.

Now, if I'm totally honest, there might have been a little bit of competition driving me to write the book as well. Early in our initial separation, Rob shared with me that he was writing a book and wanted my help in getting it published. The next thing I knew, he'd finished the book before I'd even gotten started.

That rascal beat me to it!

So yes, that probably put a bit of fire under me to get started on my book.

More than anything, though, I was ready to get back out on the speaking circuit. The book allowed me to refresh my message. After all, the car business was only a temporary fix to address my financial shortfalls. Yes, I knew that going back on the road would be met with opposition. The greater my sales, the more management wanted me on the lot. I was a top salesperson for the company many months over. In fact, I was the only woman out of a group of twenty salesmen. I was clearly holding my own, but that was never going to be enough for me. I saw this book as my liberation from that space, and that's exactly what it was.

I called in sick one day to attend a speaking engagement. Unbeknownst to me, the event planner ran radio ads to promote the event, and of all the people who could have heard it, my sales manager did. He called me in on that Friday and fired me. Thank God, my books had arrived that Monday. The following Saturday was the book release party at the Shreveport Yacht Club. It felt like the coming of a new season. The future looked brighter than it had in years.

ROB

I can't say that I was completely over the divorce. It still hurt. But a shift was taking place within me. Instead of going numb and turning away from the pain as I had done for so long, I was now turning *into* it as a head-on attempt to engage my hurt and with it my healing. I had returned to Bible College after a brief break and landed in a marriage and family counseling class that transformed my life. The timing could not have been better. I had a whole semester to study and discuss relationships, marriages in particular, in a setting that was quite therapeutic for me. Taking that class allowed me to better understand what Fox was going through, and I realized I needed to give her space.

Even more, the class brought me a level of peace. I had finally found answers to a lot of the questions that I had been searching for, particularly the questions I had about the divorce. I finally understood that Fox and I were one train with two parts, each needing to go in different directions. At some point, we were going to have to disconnect. But I was always certain that whatever the disconnect looked like, we needed to define it so that neither one of us would pull each other back to a place that the other didn't want to be. That was always the hard part.

FOX AND ROB

Defining our relationship was so critical at that moment because we were still parents. Fox was still bringing the boys to see Rob. Our children didn't need to absorb whatever tension existed between us because of the separation. We never wanted to lie to them. It was imperative for our survival that they saw us as a united front. We wanted them to know that their mother was always going to hold their father down, and he was always going to do the same to support her, whatever that might look like. The singular thing that brought peace and ease to both of us during this period was the understanding that before Fox and Rob had ever been anything, we had been friends. We would always be friends.

FOX

In 2010, just two years after our divorce was finalized, something major happened—I'd met someone. And not just any someone. My someone was a district attorney in an entirely different parish from where Rob's case was held. The funny part is when he first arrived on the scene, I welcomed him, thinking he would be someone who could help me get Rob home. If anyone knows how to get someone out of this system, it would be the person who puts them in. I started thinking about how our legal fight might benefit from his knowledge base. In the end though, I got more than I bargained for.

It was foolish of me not to see his intentions. I was vulnerable. And his generosity and humor were a welcomed reprieve.

Four out of the five boys were happy. They were living a life they'd never had before. He was showering them with gifts, toys, treats, and fun rides in big trucks. They were appeased.

Remington, however, was not with any of it. He was a junior in high school and my number one teammate. He had always been the man of the house. So there was plenty of discomfort and friction between us during this time. A part of me was challenged that he couldn't see that moving on from his father was maybe the best thing for my heart and mind. Another part of me was proud that our love had such an impact on him. We were still a family in his eyes. He was right. We were—just not in the way that we had been before, and this was unacceptable for him.

ROB

It came out of nowhere. Scratch that. It came from some-where. Just not from Fox's mouth. It came from my friend Curtis, who was also serving time at Angola and was seeing April, a woman who Fox used to share rides to Angola with for events and visit days. I did not know April prior to com-ing to prison, but she must have told Curtis after hearing from Fox herself.

FOX

Yes, April and I kind of became a twosome. We had history, too, as old high school classmates. In order to offset some of the costs of travel, we'd ride down together for events. It was great to have someone to talk to in those early hours of the morning, or the late nights if we came for a banquet or a nighttime visit. She became a kind of confidante. She was always an avid supporter of Rob and me staying together.

ROB

I had already heard that Fox had gotten a new house and was driving a drop-top Benz. Again, I didn't hear it from Fox but from Curtis. Fox and I had scaled back in our communication outside of a few letters here and there. But clearly, Fox was sharing some of what she was going through with April, and April was telling Curtis. *Okay*, I thought. *She's doing well for herself. Good. That means the boys are doing well too.* But then talks of an engagement surfaced. I honestly didn't know how to hold that information. It didn't feel good to find this out secondhand, especially from Curtis, who was the same brother who'd told me that Fox was eventually going to leave me anyway.

It felt messy, but I always wondered if this was the way things were supposed to be when you were no longer married to someone. She didn't really owe me anything in terms of what she bought or who she was dating. None of it was my business. Yet I couldn't help but feel betrayed by it all, even if that was terribly unreasonable on my part. In my mind, we were only divorced on paper. I had not divorced her in my heart, and I didn't know if I ever could.

Plus, I had been incarcerated for over a decade at this point. Fox had been there. She had always been there. She was still showing up for me. There's no way I could call it a real betrayal, even if it felt that way. After all, I was the one who brought up divorce in the first place, if only to release her from the burden of care for my situation, which was how

I had seen it at the time. It was one thing to leave me. It was another to leave me and move on to someone else. And a district attorney?!

Whew!

Fox and I had remained friends though; and after some time, she began to confide in me again.

She revealed to me the highs and lows of this relationship, and my heart broke all over again. I knew the love she deserved, even if I couldn't be the one to give it to her. I had hoped that she would have found someone genuinely amazing who would adore her and treat her like a queen.

"What are you hoping for? Do you think his bad behavior is going to stop? Do you really believe he is going to marry you, or is he stringing you along?"

I could tell she was gnawing on it. But it wasn't enough for her to leave the situation immediately. It would take much, much more.

―――――

Once every year or so, through a program called Malachi Dads, Angola would host these events where we could invite our kids to the prison to visit during the daytime. It was an outside fair with all types of activities like face painting and dunking booths. I'd signed up for Malachi Dads which had partnered with the Awana association to serve as a gap filler for incarcerated parents. They created events and experiences that would allow fathers who were incarcerated to spend time with their children. They would send buses all around the country to pick up children and bring them to the prisons.

On one of these days, my boys Remi and Lawrence were

coming, and I was so excited. Fox dropped them off at the pickup location in Shreveport at 4:30 a.m., and they were bused into Angola where the other fathers and I were allowed to greet them at the front gate when they came in. It didn't take long for Remi to express his anger and frustration about Fox's new *friend*.

I knew that Remington was feeling this change deeply. While I was gone, he was the man of the house. My nickname for him has always been my "main man." Since the divorce, he had become my primary connection to the family. I wanted to have a balanced view of the situation. I didn't want to impede Fox's freedom. But I did share Remi's concerns about this person's intentions.

If we'd put Remi in the position of being the man of the house, then I believed that he had every right to voice his opinion if someone in the household was being disrespected. To Fox's chagrin, that's exactly what Remington did. After Fox told the boys she had called it off between them, the next time the dude showed up at the house, Remi raised hell and demanded Fox's friend leave. Our love was so important that, even when we could not protect it, others around us stepped in. Remi believed in our family and was willing to do everything in his power to keep his parents from making the biggest mistake ever.

Fox wasn't happy about any of this.

FOX

Hell no, I wasn't happy about it. I'd never witnessed my son act that way. He was clearly fed up with the way my dating life had placed a deeper strain on our family. I knew I could handle myself, but seeing how angry Remi was forced me to deepen my resolve. *This thing is too complicated. I know it is, Lord. But for the first time in my life, I have help on this journey which I have been left to fend for us all on my own.* And make no mistake about it, there were times I questioned myself. *Am I doing the right thing for my children and me?*

I knew the answer to that before I even asked the question. I was always going to keep my kids first. And not just their material well-being either. Their hearts and souls mattered just as much. I didn't want another one of my bad choices to change their trajectory.

Within nine months, my entanglement was over. Through that experience, I gained a deeper appreciation for my family just the way it was. The institution of family is greater and more important than any of its individual members. *Yes, it may be an incarcerated family, but it's mine.*

ROB

This whole season in our lives was probably the most transformational for me. Hard, but life-changing, nonetheless. After the divorce, I tried finding creative ways to elevate my story and gain the support of whoever I needed to within the system. I was still very much trying to fight my way back home, but I also needed to raise the money necessary to do so. One such way was the Angola Prison Rodeo.

The Angola Prison Rodeo is the longest running prison rodeo in the nation. It got its start in 1965, and the first arena was a structure built by a handful of dedicated incarcerated persons and prison personnel. It wasn't much back then, I'm told, but by 2010, it was considered the wildest show in the South—a weekly event held every Sunday in the month of October. The rodeo's sole objective was to promote offender welfare. And as a prison trustee, I was allowed to freely interact with the outside public. I decided to use the event as an opportunity to make some money, as the proceeds from the sale of handcrafted goods were put in the offender's account.

So I decided to sell cans.

Yes, cans!

As an artistic endeavor, I took Coke cans that we were stockpiling in the dorm for recycling purposes, emptied and cleaned them out, and used what I learned in the graphic design program to recreate a small image of Sesame Street's Oscar the Grouch. I then hired some of the brothers in the dorm—paying them in cigarettes—to help with putting the labels on the cans. The label read, "Like Oscar, I'm Grouchy and Stuck in the Can." Inside of the can was a tiny paper scroll with inspirational words from a poem I'd written called "The Can" (a euphemism for prison, like "slammer" or "big house").

When people arrived and began walking the rodeo grounds, marveling at the arts and crafts on display, I'd give them my spiel and then they'd ask me how much the cans cost.

"Well, how much is it worth?" they'd ask.

"Well, I don't know. How much is it worth to you?" I'd respond.

I figured why lock myself into one price when someone might consider paying more which, in turn, would counter anyone who offered very little.

"If it's only worth a nickel to you, write the pay slip out for a nickel." (No actual cash could be exchanged. Instead, an offender filled out a carbon-copied slip that was given to the customer who then made the payment to the cashier/officer on duty.)

"If it's worth a hundred dollars to you, write the pay slip out for a hundred dollars."

I have to say, it was a great first day! I left the rodeo that day with $700 in my account and had four more Sundays during that October to do it again.

It was those little victories that got my juices flowing again. My imagination had been rebooted from the relational funk I was in, and I was ready to do more.

FOX AND ROB

And *more* doesn't even begin to describe what we did next. Fox had gotten Rob a subscription to *Runner's World* magazine because running had been an outlet for her while in prison. Rob would send her letters with exercise workouts she could do since her facility didn't have a gym. Whenever she was free to move about outside, she'd run in order to move some of the stress and anxiety she was feeling out of her body. Running was also something that served her well during her time on active duty in the navy. This sparked an idea! We were both noticing the devastating results experienced by incarcerated men and women who were not taking care of their health—at least as much as they could in that environment. Diabetes, high blood pressure, and other illnesses were abundant. Fox first suggested starting a running club in women's prisons. Rob pushed that idea further with marathons.

ROB

I was reading an article one day in *Runner's World* about a group of women in a Midwestern prison who were running for a cause. They'd gotten the warden of the facility's approval to run around the interior of the prison to raise money. There was also a segment of the magazine where the editors would shout out to people who were coming up with creative ways to implement a running lifestyle. Immediately, the light bulb went off.

When Fox came to visit again, I said, "Man, I think we need to find a cause to run for."

"A cause? Running? What do you mean?"

"I think we can use this as a campaign to bring greater awareness to something we care about while simultaneously helping me raise awareness about our matter with those who might help me get released."

It just clicked. Fox had been talking a lot about the impact incarceration has on the children of the incarcerated. She was seeing firsthand the challenges with our own boys and was frustrated by how often children had to pay for their parents' transgressions.

We had a cause!

FOX

I'd seen it with my own eyes! Not just with our kids but with the children of people around us. These babies were basically set on a trajectory to failure all because one parent or both parents were locked up. I'd already begun working with another organization at the time that could offer us the statistics and data to make the case of this campaign. Rob and I thought, *Maybe people don't give a damn about us, the incarcerated, as human beings; but maybe, just maybe, they might care about the children and feel like they are worth saving.*

ROB

"Fox, you should run a marathon."

You can imagine how Fox looked at me. Incredulous doesn't even begin to describe it.

"As a matter of fact, you aren't going to run one marathon," I continued. "You should run *seven*."

FOX

This man was out of his mind.

And I loved it!

Of course, I'd never even run a half-marathon at that time, but just call us overachievers when it comes to these bright ideas of ours.

The number seven wasn't random.

Children of incarcerated parents are seven times more likely to end up in prison themselves. Plus, Rob was going to coordinate a simultaneous run inside of Angola. I was running outside, representing the children, and he and others were running inside, representing the parents.

And we were off!

ROB

The timing for this couldn't have been better. One of our city's representatives was walking from Shreveport to the capital of Louisiana, Baton Rouge, for autism. We knew that if we wanted the world to know our cause, and ultimately our story, then this was a great way to get it out into the world. Our plan was to run seven marathons in 2011, but Fox would begin her training and do a test run at the 2010 Thanksgiving half-marathon in Shreveport.

FOX

Listen, the most I'd probably ever run at one time in my entire life was five miles, and it had been a decade since that. This wasn't going to be easy. I didn't have a formal trainer. I was still working and pursuing my own dreams as a speaker and now author.

I'm going to do it for the children.

With every step, I understood my purpose.

I'm going to do it for the children.

With every step, I understood my assignment.

I'm going to do it for the children.

With every single step, I understood that we were doing something that was bigger than us.

That was probably the only reason why I didn't quit. I knew what was happening to these babies. I was doing it for them.

My first official marathon for the campaign was the Rock 'n' Roll Marathon on February 2, 2011, in New Orleans.

Rob's run was going to run simultaneously at Angola. We were going to start at the same time.

As the coordinator of the Angola marathon, Rob was able to get organizations inside the prison to join his vision of running for a cause. Outside of the prison though, I ran the remaining six races in marathons all over the country, including the Tyler Rose Marathon in Tyler, Texas; the Big D Marathon in Dallas, Texas; and the Louisiana Trials Marathon, just to name a few. All seven were completed in one year.

What I enjoyed most about the experience was the comradery and support that came from the fellow runners. That was the most encouraging group of people I had ever encountered in my life. Every step of the way, folks were there cheering for us and rooting us on. I also learned to never judge a book by its cover. There was an older gentleman who was clearly in his seventies or eighties next to me at the starting line. I sized him up in my mind, just knowing I would be able to beat him, if no one else. The race started, and he took off. I never saw him again until I finally made it to the finishing pool.

ROB

It wasn't hard at all to get the incarcerated men involved in the campaign. My ministry and messaging had been centered on accountability and what it meant to be good fathers to our children who were statistically in that same loop. I was constantly talking about ways we could stop the cycle. I got quite a few guys to commit to running with me that day.

It was still quite the task, though, when it came to the

actual training. Most of these men had never run for that length. Many weren't accustomed to running in any sustained way at all. I ended up going to the boxing team for training and additional participants since they already had running as part of their workout program to prepare for fights. I knew they were runners innately and got a few of them to sign up. Then I got really creative. I took the concept further by calling my inside marathon a run, walk, or crawl. That was a hilarious challenge. These men could run the distance, walk it, or yes, crawl it. After adding those options, more men signed up—sixty in total.

Imagine a sea of mostly Black and Brown men in matching T-shirts that said, "Angola ain't no place to be" (thanks to the graphic design program I graduated from) running, walking, or crawling around the massive East prison yard.

It was radical.

It was defiant.

It was a beautiful sight.

The marathons we both ran were super successful that year. They generated so much awareness for the children of the incarcerated as well as funding for programs. Fox was contracted by the Office of Juvenile Justice to teach the girls at Ware Youth Center the life skills program I had created. Other opportunities also came her way. We were creating impact and raising awareness and resources. It also was another way we were establishing ourselves as advocates and activists. Working together on this also felt like it was restoring a tiny bit of that fire that had been extinguished by the divorce and Fox's subsequent relationship.

I still needed her. Yes, to go to war alongside me. I can't deny that. It was always going to be the state of Louisiana versus Robert G. Richardson or the Louisiana Department of Corrections and Parole Board versus Robert G. Richardson until the day I could walk free. But I suspect that I needed her in other ways. Ways I was somewhat scared to unpack. Fox has always unlocked something inside of me. I could have given up long ago. But as much as I wanted liberty for myself, I wanted liberty for her. I wanted to be free to love her the way she always deserved to be loved.

But the first step was getting freed.

It had been almost nine years since I'd petitioned for post-conviction relief after my sentence was held up on my appeal. My matter had sat for that long before the judge decided to rule on it in 2011.

Unfortunately, I was locked up at that time in solitary confinement—for a reason I never saw coming.

You see, Fox had begun to find clever ways to increase awareness of my case on this fairly new to us platform called social media. She had been gaining traction with people all over the country who were hearing about the injustice that had happened to our family. She'd even posted an interview with our sons as a way to open up the dialogue about the children of the incarcerated. We both believed that with the help of the community, we could actually raise awareness about these tertiary victims of incarceration—children.

Apparently, the prison felt like Fox's posts amounted to misrepresentation of me to the public and warranted sending me to Camp J lockdown—the worst segment of solitary confinement. It's essentially a dungeon. They had to manually pump sunlight or daylight into the space in order for me to see anything. The most painful part of this experience was when my family first visited me under these conditions and had to bear witness to the next level of dehumanization happening in that institution. Fox and the boys had to walk through this part of the compound and see men held in what amounted to kennels—a 12 × 6 × 8 dog cage for human beings.

The guards brought Fox and the boys to a caged holding space and locked the door behind them. There, I sat across from them, behind Plexiglas and chicken wire, handcuffed, shackled. I imagine I looked horrifying to them as I had no rights to groom myself, and daily showers were not allowed. Upon seeing me, the boys started sobbing loudly. They were heartbroken. They couldn't touch me with the glass between us. When I saw their wet faces, I intentionally slid out of the handcuffs and showed them my hands.

"They can't hold me," I said. I had to somehow let them know that I wasn't going to let this place break me, nor us. I was still in control.

The prison's retaliation only fueled me. I used the nine months of darkness to refine my arguments. In my mind, I was six years shy of 20/45 eligibility. Whether they gave me post-conviction relief or not—which they didn't as the judge ruled against it—I was setting my eyes on 2017, when I would finally be eligible.

By federal law, every jail must develop a clear prisoner grievance procedure, including a formal means of delivering complaints and concerns from a prisoner to the administration and steps by which a written response is given. So I filed a grievance for myself and another gentleman who had a similar situation regarding our 20/45 parole eligibility. This was the first step to establish eligibility. When the man's paperwork came back saying that he was eligible, I knew it had worked. He'd caught his charge around the same time I did, so I was feeling really good about my chances. Since the district court had denied my post-conviction relief, this was my only legal redress to the courts.

FOX

I'd gotten confirmation that Rob's grievance was sound from, of all people, *the* district attorney. In fact, I'd started sharing what Rob was doing with a number of people, including the attorney. I gave the paperwork to him with the hope of seeing whether Rob had a legitimate legal issue. Regardless of how he might have felt about my continued support of Rob, he had to admit that the argument was well written. He said that the grievance had substance to it.

That's all we needed to hear.

ROB

That's the nature of war, right? You win a battle, then you lose a battle, then you win again. In the end, hopefully you have more wins than losses so you can win the war. I'd lost the appeal but gained the possibility of a pardon. Then I'd lost the possibility of a pardon but gained the possibility of post-conviction relief. Then I'd lost post-conviction relief and was now looking for the overall win with 20/45. This gave my case, and us, new life.

In the meantime, I returned to finishing Bible College after another brief pause. I wanted to have my degree completed and a number of certifications under my belt whenever opportunity knocked. The last thing I wanted to do was be afforded an opportunity and not be able to take advantage of it.

I didn't realize it then, but in hindsight I wanted to be someone Fox found worthy of it all.

FOX

I think I understood that too. Finally. No matter what, Rob was home to me. He was my sanctuary. I'd come to the point where I didn't want to move forward anymore without us at least trying to work things out.

"I want to come home," I said to him.

"What does that mean?" he replied.

"Honestly, I don't know," I said.

And I didn't know. I just knew that we needed a fresh start. No matter what storms of life swirled around us, no matter our next move, we could only find our calm with each other.

"Okay," he said.

"Okay."

Even as we were trying to put our relationship back together, change was on the horizon. I knew that when Remington graduated from high school in May 2011, and headed off to attend Xavier University in New Orleans, it was time for the boys and me to move out of Shreveport. If we were ever going to be able to climb to the next rung of success as a family, we would need more than the city could offer. I also thought that adding "Dr." to my name would enhance my chances of expanding my speaking tour and add more credibility to my voice. If I could go from the second to last poorest state in the country to one of the wealthier states in the country and be successful, then I would be paving a way for my boys to follow suit. So, I applied and was accepted into the PhD program at Texas Southern University in the Administration of Justice program.

The boys and I moved to Houston, Texas, and began to make a life there. It was a new beginning for all of us.

13

WIND BENEATH
OUR WINGS

We are not here to fix, change or belittle another person. We
are here to support, forgive and heal one another.

Marianne Williamson, *A Return to Love*

FOX

The drive from Houston to Angola was just an hour
longer than the drive from Shreveport. Ironically, in
addition to offering me a clean slate, the move to
Houston brought Rob and me closer together. We had come
to terms with the fact that we were stronger together than
we were apart, and even though we refrained from labels for
our return to love, it was clear that he was my home because
he was where my heart was.

This new distance between us meant that we had to really focus on what we wanted and needed from each other, how we would choose to support each other, and how we would move past all that had led to the division in the first place. We were relearning how to care for ourselves and finding space to better care for each other. The truth is, when it came to the dissolution of our marriage, we were both just trying to make the best decisions that we could at that moment. Whatever capacity we held to care for ourselves and each other we wielded to survive the situation we were in. And we couldn't hold those limited capacities against each other.

Another piece of it was much simpler to me. I've always known that Robert cared about me. It was never a question. It was in the big things, the large sacrifices he made, yes. But it was also in the little things he would do. Pulling out my chair. Opening my door. Seeing if I needed anything. He made sure I ate before he would eat himself. It was just his way.

So in all that I was doing to take care of the boys and figuring out how I was going to get the next paycheck or the next speaking contract, I found myself still being able to speak with Rob and share my heart. And that mattered so much to me. Sometimes I even felt guilty about it. Because at least I was free, right? There I was, laying all of my weight on him, and this brother was living in hell. There were times when I felt like the little, menial things I was going through couldn't compare to his life in captivity. And yet, he never made me feel like I couldn't bring my hardships to him. He never made me feel like I couldn't need him. I just needed to make myself vulnerable enough to accept his support.

Rob has a calm and peaceful energy that can only come from God. It's part of his aura. When we were going through some of the most tumultuous life battles, he was always steady. Even in all the madness and chaos, he was able to find some calm, some connection to God, in order to stay centered.

I believed him that day in 1999, when we were both sitting at a table in the courthouse, dressed in prison garb, seeing each other for the first time since our worlds fell apart. Terrified, I said to him, "Maybe my mama was right. Maybe two people this much alike don't need to be together. I mean, I love you, but maybe we just keep making bad choices together."

Rob turned to me, looked me right in my eyes while holding my hand tight, and said, "We're going to be alright."

I believed him. And in the most honest moments with myself, I still did.

ROB

Of the few memories I have of my mother, there are a couple that really defined what love is. My mother was not just my mom who loved me but she was my friend. That's a piece that is sometimes missing in our parenting. We forget that our children are human beings who not only want to rely on us for nurturing and discipline but who want us to really like them as people. That was a gift my mother gave me. Love and friendship. Good or bad, she would talk to me about the problems she and my dad were having. She taught me how to comb my hair, and she'd let me comb hers.

We even learned how to drive a car together. Yes, I was in kindergarten, but she would sit me in the passenger seat of the car my dad bought her, and she'd drive around with me, being as careful as she possibly could. My dad's mode of teaching was this, "The only way you are going to learn how to drive is if you get in the car. This is the brake. This is the gas. Go for it." And that's what she did. There would be days when she'd take me with her, and we'd just hang out.

Then she was gone. And I was in this space where I was forced to live without my mother, yes, but also without my first friend. So, when I popped up on Fox's doorstep that day so many years ago, I knew exactly what I was feeling. It was a connection. Something deep down inside of me pushed its way to the surface and the emotion that showed up, it was familiar. I wanted more of it. And over the course of space and time, Fox and I carved a friendship out of our love and passion for one another. As intense as our sexual energy could be, it was the friendship that took root because we spent so much time not in each other's space. Sometimes, she was in another relationship or I was. Even with me being in prison for so long, the vast majority of our relationship was long-distance, so we had no choice but to develop a comradery above our attraction. We got to know each other on a different level through heart-to-heart talks and letters because there was no other way to express ourselves. We bonded together in ways that romantic love alone could never bond people.

Our friendship is why many of our previous relationships couldn't stand. Fox's ex, Lawrence's father, couldn't understand why she could not go a day without talking to me. My ex, Mahlik's mother, couldn't understand why I couldn't go a day without talking to Fox. Why I kept going back to Louisiana. And any other person who has been in our lives was always saying, "Why do y'all have to be around each other like this?"

FOX AND ROB

The truth is, we've fallen in and out of love over the thirty-five years we've been in each other's lives. In the Greek language, there are several meanings of love. The most common ones that show up in biblical translations are *eros* (erotic/sensual love), *phileo* (brother/sisterly affection), and *agape* (unconditional/godly love). Our eros love has waned at times. But it has been our phileo and agape love that have kept us connected. And the regular distances we've had over the years have helped us refine all of that love. From the letter-writing days when Fox would record sweet messages to Rob on cassette tapes complete with music playing in the background to now, as we stand beside each other in our freedom, working to help other families become free.

FOX

I think moving to Houston also helped me get back into my own space so I could hear clearly what the next move should be for the children, and for Rob and his case, and for myself. I'd already decided that Rob and I were going to make it. Period. There were no other options for us. Needless to say, not many people agreed with that decision. My mother, in particular, had a different perspective on my relationship with Rob. When she and I lived together, before my move to Houston, I remember telling her that when Rob came home, he was coming to move in with us. We were going to be a family again.

"Oh, he's not going to live here," she said.

Well, that's all I needed to hear. If she didn't want to live with him, fine. But I knew then that I had to find another place for my children and me. Off to Houston we went!

When we arrived in Texas, the first thing I did, besides registering for the PhD program at Texas Southern, was start working in the car business again. Except this time, it was with my cousin who owned his own car lot in Houston. It was a business I knew, and it provided a stream of income that didn't require any steep learning curves.

Remington was away at Xavier University and was majoring in premed. I was so proud of him. He'd escaped the system's planned trajectory for him. And the other four boys—Lawrence, Freedom, Justus, and little Robert—were very active in the dealership. The big boys would go to auctions and buy cars. They also washed and cleaned them to be showcased. All the boys would do what I called "street corner marketing." They'd pass out flyers and business cards to neighboring businesses. It was a family affair, for sure. As it always has been. We still had work to do, though, to be truly together in all the ways that really mattered. Rob was still serving a practical life sentence. Time was passing, and we were inching closer to his eligibility date for the 20/45 parole law. By moving to Texas, I was expanding my network and gathering additional resources so we could hire a lawyer to help us through this next phase of the process.

ROB

After I left Camp J and solitary confinement for all the social media awareness, I was moved to an outer camp. This was like a disciplinary camp and the next step toward getting back into the main prison. It was a process to return. Kind of a decompression they put us through. First, when we came out of isolation lockdown, we went to a disciplinary camp. From there, we worked our way back into population (the main prison), which is where I needed to be.

And I didn't want to wait forever to get there.

Being in the main prison versus disciplinary camp is like the difference between being in New York City and the rest of the world. The main prison is the central area of operations for the prison. It's where the education building is. It's where all the trades and rehabilitative programming happen. It's also where the law library is. If one were trying to go home, disciplinary camp is not where they would want to be. And certainly not isolation.

Normally, it was really hard to leave one of the disciplinary camps and get back to the main prison. This was because we had to get someone to approve our being moved from one camp to another. These changes usually were aligned with job changes where we were being asked to go from one field line to another. But I figured out another route that might make the move even easier and didn't require approval.

I put in a request for a dorm change.

There was a Black warden named Kevin Benjamin who seemed to have some degree of compassion and empathy for us. Interestingly enough, he'd been promoted through the ranks at Angola, and in a way, we'd come up through the prison system together, even if on different sides. I ran into him one day and decided to shoot my shot.

"Hey, man! How long have you been back here?" he asked.

I told him a bit about what happened and how I ended

up in the disciplinary camp and for how long. He stared at me intently for a long while, then quietly asked, "What can I do to get you back to the main prison?"

There it was.

"Well," I said, "I need to get back up there fast because I need to get into the law library and finish my arguments."

"Let me see what I can do," he said. "But you are still going to have to get somebody to approve the move. I don't have the authority."

I was ready for that.

"Yeah, but you *do* have the authority to approve a dorm change. That's really all I'm asking for, right?"

He looked at me and laughed good and long.

"You know what? That just might work!"

He put the paperwork in, and before the day had ended, the guards called me and told me to pack my stuff because I was moving to Walnut 4, bed 40, Field Line Seven.

In the main prison.

Once I got to the main prison, I went straight to the law library. I needed to know as much as I could about the 20/45 law.

I studied, meditated, and Shepardized cases daily. *Shepard's* Citations allows one to track the citation history of a court, so when someone shepardizes a case, they will see all the other cases that have cited that case and whether the case was treated favorably or not. I wanted to make sure I fit into this category of people before I began the work of submitting my grievance and diving into the process. I had a sixty-year sentence for armed robbery and a couple of five-year sentences for the jury tampering charge which amounted to two separate terms. This law specifically said,

"No matter the term or terms."[1] This meant that it didn't matter how many sentences I may have had. I could have had fifty different sentences for an array of crimes that could've amounted to a thousand years, but as long as they all were numbered sentences and not *life*, I could actually make the argument to the court.

September 2017, the date I would become eligible, couldn't come fast enough. I had four years to make this happen. All the tumblers I'd been wrestling with seemed to fit, so it was just a matter of beginning the process.

In March 2013, I started what would become my first argument for 20/45.

Sixty days later, I was denied.

They don't have to give us a reason.

I would not be deterred though. This gave me an opportunity to appeal that denial at the next level, which is exactly what I did.

At the second level, the appeal went to the secretary of the Department of Corrections. I basically voiced my same opinion in writing. I explained to the department secretary that I was being denied parole consideration in violation of the law. I cited the relevant law that applied to my case.

In less than forty-five days, I was denied yet again!

Again! Without explanation!

Clearly, they wanted me to quit. There was only one of two options at that point. I could either let the appeal die or pay the court costs to file the complaint in civil court. The action would then become a civil issue, even though it's a criminal issue at its root.

FOX

Now I needed to figure out how I was going to file this for Rob, considering that I didn't have much money that wasn't tied up in the expenses of our family. Rob claimed he had money in his prison account and said he wanted to take it from there.

"What money? You don't even have any savings," I said.

"Yes, I do," he answered. "I make four cents an hour, but they only give me two cents. They put the other two cents into a savings account. That money accumulates over space and time, and in the event I get discharged one day, they will turn that over to me in exchange for my good time."

"Okay, so how does that help us?" I asked.

"There's another way you can access the money. You can use that account for legal and educational reasons. I think this qualifies as a legal reason, right?"

It surely did.

ROB

I petitioned the prison to allow me to use the money for a legal matter that I was filing in civil court. They granted me access to the money, and we were able to file it in court, which cost us $485.

As determined as I was, I couldn't help but think about all the hoops I was jumping through and how the system makes it so hard for people to file merit issues. Our grievances too often fall on deaf ears, and too many people give up on the pursuit of release because they don't have the support I had.

FOX

The only way that I was going to be able to help Rob at this stage was to come up with more money for an attorney who could help with the post-conviction matter that we were fighting on another front.

So, I sold my car.

Yes, that drop-top Benz.

Remington was so angry about that. He was away at college, and because of our financial situation, I was rarely able to send him money. When he found out that I was selling the car to help his father with another attorney, he was livid. It's not that he didn't want his father out of jail—he absolutely did. He was just concerned about how many sacrifices I'd made, and he and his brothers had made, to try to make that happen.

But he was going to have to stay mad about it.

Because, by this point, I was singularly focused on getting our family back together. And no matter how long it took, I was in it for the long haul.

Rob had proven, even in our more challenging times together, he would always show up the best he could. He would always take whatever tools he had and do what needed to be done. I appreciated him for being unstoppable. We were both out there being concerned about freedom and family. But that weighed heavier on Rob. He was challenged by having these seemingly insurmountable odds stacked against him on a daily basis. To live under a cloud of uncertainty all the time had to be beyond hard.

Unfortunately, the lawyer I'd hired, Elton Richie, couldn't see that. Two weeks out from the filing deadline, and after paying him $15,000 to work on Rob's case, he sent us a letter in the mail stating there was nothing further he could do for us. The post-conviction was dead in the water.

Just like that.

He took our money and gave us nothing more than a list of billable hours.

ROB

After his firm ditched us, I realized that if the argument for my release under 20/45 was going to be made, it was going to have to be made by me. It didn't seem like anyone else understood the dynamics of the argument I was trying to make, so I crafted it myself. Then I tested it.

I'd already started a social justice ministry in the prison. Instead of trying to lead people to the Lord—the prison had other ministers who drove in that lane—I was trying to lead people to the law.

I'm going to leave the salvation part up to God and get people free another way.

I couldn't save these men. But I could possibly teach them how to get out of this particular condition.

I would go from one yard to the next, talking to people who were fixed with a similar sentence to mine.

"Listen, I know you don't understand this argument," I said. "But I'm going to ask you to help pay for a lawyer to help us all out."

I did another call out program where I invited men who I'd identified as having the same potential for 20/45 eligibility as me to watch me debate three of our best jailhouse lawyers. I provided refreshments sponsored by another one of the groups.

When the men arrived, I began debating the law RS: 15:574.4(A)(2) with a guy named Arthur Carter. I did the same with another gentleman we called Big L.A. and another man named Kerry Myers. All these men were considered well-known legal minds inside Angola prison. I challenged them to argue against the law, as each of them believed that the law did not apply to those of us convicted after January 1, 1997. It was there that I perfected my argument in favor of the law as it was originally written.

Kerry probably gave me the most formidable argument, because he was good friends with the lawyer who had basically made the law a moot issue for those of us who had applied in the first place. Apparently, I was convincing enough that a few of the guys waited around after the debate to find out more about how to move forward.

"Well, we need a lawyer. I can make the argument, but we need a lawyer to stand with me. And I can't pay for one. If you want in on this, how much do each of you have on a lawyer?"

"I have $1,500," one man said.

"I can put up $500," another man said.

"My mama is coming to visit this weekend, so maybe if you can share what you've shared with us with her, I can cosign, and we can get more money."

That's exactly what I did. Alfred Bankston's mother (the same man I'd filed a grievance for earlier) flew in from Florida and drove an hour to Angola from Baton Rouge. When she arrived, I went into the A Building area and visited with her for about an hour and a half. After explaining everything to her, she said, "Well, baby, I don't know a whole lot about what you're talking about, but I get the feeling that *you* know what you're talking about. Whatever it is that the lawyer wants to charge y'all for this, I got half of it."

Half! The woman had just said she'd pay for half our attorney fees! My heart leapt in my chest.

"Just tell me where I need to send the money to because I need my baby home," she said.

Mama Bev, as she is affectionately known, spoke the words that were the wind beneath my wings.

I called Fox and told her the good news. She immediately took to social media to see if she could get the attention of a lawyer who might understand the civil issue.

FOX AND ROB

We were on our way. The energy around our visits at this time was charged. Hope had enlivened us in a way that we hadn't seen or felt in a very long time. It was beautiful. And on top of all of that, the boys were getting older, and Fox was contemplating her next move. She'd gotten Lawrence into college early. Instead of doing his senior year in high school, she was able to enroll him in a dual-enrollment program. Lawrence completed high school at the end of his junior year and started college at Prairie View A&M University in June. The twins were headed to high school, and little Robert was in second grade. If there was ever a time for us to make another shift, hopefully even a final one, it was now.

FOX

I'd already made a commitment to Rob and our family. If I was going to be in this for the long haul, if I was going to get my husband—my children's father—home, then I needed to be back in Louisiana. More than money, we needed proximity. To get Rob's issues resolved, I was going to have to be closer to him. I could not save my family from all the way in Texas. By March 2014, I shared this with Rob.

"I want to move back to Louisiana," I said.

"Move back? Really?"

"Yeah, I'm just realizing that the only way I'm going to get you home is if I've got boots on the ground. I can't do it from over here."

I'd tried going to school. I'd moved there to go to school. But after my second semester of working on my PhD with two kids in college and three kids at home, maintaining that workload with no family around was not sustainable, financially or otherwise. I needed to dedicate the hours I was putting in at school to working instead. Working to make money for our family. And working on Rob's case. Even more than at any other point in my life, my first order of business was putting my family back together. Freedom was now this family's business.

The boys and I moved to New Orleans on June 1, 2014. We were all positioning ourselves for Rob's return home no matter how long it would take, and we knew that there were freedom warriors in the Crescent City. After posting on social media that we needed a civil lawyer, we finally got a hit. A young woman named Ashley Greenhouse reached out and recommended her legal partner Ronald S. Haley Jr. She said that he would be ideal for the case.

God was in this! Do you hear me?

True to her word, Mrs. Greenhouse made the connection between her law partner and us immediately. After we hired

Ron, I asked Mrs. Greenhouse in passing how she knew me. At first, it made sense. She was from Shreveport, and I knew her mother. Then it made even more sense.

Her grandfather was Mr. Johnson, the angel of a man who, over a decade prior, headed up the GED program in the women's prison and helped me transition into the halfway house. I had absolutely no idea the world could be so small. But God did.

ROB

On top of everything, Ron Haley Jr. would later go on to handle some of the biggest police brutality cases in the state of Louisiana, including the Ronald Greene case that would be the impetus for the US Justice Department to launch a federal investigation into the Louisiana State Police for beatings of mostly Black men. It's been beautiful to watch his work evolve and know that we were at the genesis of it.

After getting Ron on the phone, he said, "I'll need half to get started."

Well, I know I got half for sure.

Fox helped facilitate his payment from my friend's mother, and once that was squared away, Ron came to Angola for a visit.

At first glance, he didn't seem like a formidable presence. He was young, jovial, and confident—but for no apparent reason, I thought. He definitely contrasted the sharp-edged characters I was used to encountering on this journey. I could tell he came from a loving family because, while he was a powerful attorney, he was a very compassionate and empathetic person. When he walked in, I shook his hand, and we walked to the area of the visiting room where lawyers can meet with their clients. I explained to him what I was hoping to accomplish, and he assured me that he understood. But he was still a businessman.

"I see the name on the check I received. Is the other payment coming from her?" Ron asked.

"No, the other payment will be coming from different sources," I replied.

Then I explained what I'd been able to put together with the other men in the prison.

"Oh, so you've pulled a consortium of people together in support of this argument? That's brilliant! I like that!"

From there, we got down to work. It probably took Ron all of maybe three visits and four phone calls for us to really get the argument in place to the point where he could speak to it as much as I could. Then he made a major move in the process. As a licensed attorney, he came with a bar roll number which would ensure that the application was processed instead of just filed.

FOX

And by "filed," Rob means dumped in the trash can. There had already been an investigation into the Fifth Circuit Court in Gretna, Louisiana, where clerk Jerrold Peterson died by suicide in his office after writing a letter confessing how he and his office had destroyed writ applications filed by people without attorneys. We knew crooked things were happening, so we needed protection against that. Ron helped us do just that. He got our filing advanced to the next step.

ROB

And the next step for us was to wait for the court to call a hearing where Ron and I filed a joint argument that allowed me to be in the courtroom with him.

When we entered the court that day, I held a mixture of hope and trepidation in my heart. This was the place where we would express the argument that I'd been developing for years at this point. Finally, someone was going to listen. No one-word denials. Today, they would see my face. They had to hear me out.

When Commissioner Nicole Robinson allowed us to bring the argument forth, Ron stumbled some. After all, he had been given a crash course in this argument and had not spent years on it like I had. But I knew that if he lacked a command for it, that might mean that the judge could lack an interpretation to apply to it. I'd come too far to be there and couldn't let that happen.

I had two options: I could stay still and say nothing, or I could blurt out and hope that she saw me. Because I was shackled and chained, I couldn't really raise my hand. I tried leaning over, hoping that she'd see me with my one Baptist pointer finger sticking up just above the table line. When she didn't, I just spoke up. I could tell that everyone in the court was baffled by my interjection, but, at that point, I didn't care. Ron was being outmatched by the opposing counsel arguing on behalf of the attorney general's office.

My life was dependent on this. It was our only way out.

"Excuse me, Your Honor, may I speak?"

FOX

When this man said, "Excuse me, Your Honor, may I speak?"
. . . It was glorious! I just knew it was game over.

Our sons and I had walked in that courtroom with so
much pride. Clean from head to toe. I was dressed like the
traditional Southern belle with a big floppy hat, a long strand
of pearls, and a linen swing dress with modest heels. The
boys were all suited up as usual with shirts and ties from
the thrift store and fresh haircuts by yours truly. They were
going to see their daddy, so it was important to them that
they looked their best. This moment symbolized progress,
baby, and I was here for it all!

ROB

At the sound of my voice, the woman representing the Department of Corrections turned around and looked at me
over the top of her glasses with disdain. *That's okay. I know
you*, I thought. I knew that she was the daughter of Heis-
man Trophy winner and NFL great Billy Cannon, who in
the early 1980s got in trouble for counterfeiting and was
now working as a dentist in the prison. I knew that she had
no real understanding of the law. The only reason she was
in the room was nepotism. But I didn't focus on that. The
judge was going to let me speak.

I started with the history of the initial argument:

In 1974, a man by the name of Walter Burnette was convicted of breaking into the St. Tammany Parish home of
Pat O'Brien, the famed New Orleans restauranteur. He was

229

sentenced to ninety-nine years in prison. The O'Brien family never thought that Burnette would be released, considering the length of his sentence.

In 1990, the state created the 20/45 law which started out at 30/60 (meaning, those who were at least thirty years served and sixty years of age may be eligible for parole). In 2006, the litigation titled *David Tell v Richard Stalder* ended with a high court ruling in favor of Tell, another armed robber similarly situated like Burnette. Accordingly, the outcome of Tell litigation would apply to all prisoners with armed robbery convictions. The parties agreed in the Tell litigation that no appeal would be taken from the State District Court ruling in Tell and that Tell would go final. This decision gave Walter Burnette the opportunity to come before the board and petition for his release because it set a new precedent. The owners of Pat O'Brien's were livid. Keith Nordyke who had become popular in Louisiana as a parole expert, represented the plaintiff in the above-mentioned case. They won their argument and settled the matter for people like Burnette who were now eligible for parole consideration, having served twenty years and reaching the age of forty-five.

But the argument resurfaced in 2014, when the Department of Corrections unceremoniously decided to reinterpret the law yet again. But this time in the case of *Calvin Cittadino and Jerry Francis v Leblanc*. Attorney Keith Nordyke stepped in to argue for the defendants as he did before in the 2006 David Tell case. Subsequently, a deal was made at the federal level that the law would only apply to those who were *sentenced* before January 1, 1997, specifically those Nordyke was representing.

After bringing Commissioner Robinson up to speed, I specified that the argument had already been made in my favor in the original case. And it had been made in that exact same court. The outcome of that proceeding meant that Walter Burnette received relief. Why shouldn't I receive that same relief for a similar crime only decades apart?

I grounded my argument in what they called a *manifestly erroneous interpretation of law*. In effect, I was saying that the Department of Corrections' reinterpretation of the 20/45 law was intentional and deserved its own hearing.

My heart was beating a hundred beats per second, or so it felt. This was it—the address I'd been meticulously preparing for over the last few years. I took a big breath, and then I took my seat.

Commissioner Robinson took a beat before responding, "Mr. Richardson makes a pretty legitimate argument. He makes an argument at least legitimate enough to be heard further. You have thirty days to file your briefs. Counsel as well as defense. Once I get your briefs, then I'll take it under advisement, and I'll render my decision and recommendations at the end of that finding."

That was one of the happiest days of my life!

FOX

Ours too! I'll always be grateful to Commissioner Robinson. She was an angel for our family. She stood her own ground, made her own judgment, and wasn't going to be influenced by her superiors or anyone else, despite knowing that it was going to open up a floodgate.

FOX AND ROB

There wasn't any time for us to rest, though. We were too close. There could be no distractions from the task at hand. Yes, it felt good to get the green light from Commissioner Robinson, for Rob to shock the hell out of that room as he eloquently made his claim to freedom. But sometimes, when something feels too good, you'll get too comfortable and rock yourself right to sleep. And we couldn't afford that. Given just how inhumane being in that cage for that long was for Rob, we weren't going to let up. We had a singular focus. We also both understood that our relationship and what it represented to us, our boys, and the community at large was bigger than anything temporal. Our flesh would not get the best of us. We'd operate in the Spirit at all times. If we really believed that God could bring Rob home, then we had to move in knowing that and give our family's restoration our undivided attention.

14

LET THE KING KNOW
I'M HERE

Determine that the thing can and shall be done and then
. . . find the way.

Abraham Lincoln, *Abraham Lincoln:*
Speeches and Writings

FOX

I think this was probably the first time I went home and cleaned out a drawer for Rob. I bought him some new underwear, undershirts, and socks. *Come on home, baby!* I felt like I was floating.

Hope had shown its glorious face again. We were so close we could taste it. Relationally, it was still challenging—we were eighteen years into this adventure—but our renewed commitment and shared purpose had revived our love and gave us the necessary determination to stand together and make it work. Rob's heart had returned to its home—in my capable and loving hands. In addition, we were not only making headway in Rob's case but we were also realizing just how much of an impact we could make on other incarcerated families who needed us to win. Because of that, I began organizing rallies and events to bring even more awareness to the issues and challenges brought on by mass incarceration, excessive sentencing, and the overall systemic injustices found in our criminal justice system. More than anything, I think we were grounded in the intention that what God could do for us, God could use us to do for others.

ROB

I was hopeful too. But I also didn't want to count my chickens before they hatched. We had one more argument to make in the court. I'd only advanced us to the next level, to where they could hold an evidentiary hearing. The first hearing was merely a status hearing. We had been tasked with having to come up with our brief in thirty days, so once again, Ron and I began working on the argument.

The first thing we started experiencing were time delays on the side of the Department of Corrections. They kept asking for extensions because we kept piling on evidence in our favor—even all the way back to when the initial law itself was written in 1987.

I asked Fox to go to Louisiana State University, where the state held their archives, and do some digging.

FOX

"The archives? How do I do that?" I asked.

But then I did what I had always done over the years—I learned quickly, and I figured it out.

ROB

It was great because we were able to access all kinds of legislative cassette tapes, which I got transcribed. We now knew who authored the bill, and we learned that the arguments were made in the judge's chambers. We were also able to read the original interpretation of it. According to the way the law read, whenever there was a competing interest, the judge was supposed to take into consideration something called statutory construction. This simply meant that if there was a law that was in conflict with another one, the judge needed to evaluate which one came first, which came after, and which one spoke to the other one. So the opening language "notwithstanding any other law to the contrary" was where my argument found life.

FOX AND ROB

While Rob was working on the 20/45 argument, our family was working hard on other avenues. Hope had overtaken us all. There was a new governor of Louisiana who was promising to bring change to the state, and we took him at his word. There had already been a slew of justice reform bills that hit the Senate floor, so Fox was making multiple trips to the capital in order to see if she could advocate for bills that would help families of the incarcerated being put back on the legislative docket.

It was so hard though. The politicians were looking for the low-hanging fruit. They wanted to get something done fast, so they attacked the less complicated issues as opposed to the heavier issues, such as crimes of violence and people serving life terms. We worked with those issues, hoping ours would be next in line.

FOX

I spent a good portion of 2017 at the state capitol, working to get geriatric parole eligibility for people serving life. This was unpaid labor, of course, but it was for my family and many other families living in this place called Louisiana—otherwise known as the incarceration capital of the world. Unfortunately, it didn't make it out of committee. It was only April, and I was crushed. But I held on to the knowledge that when we work for the greater good of others, God will always bless our efforts. That's what we believe.

I was on my way back home from a large, sponsored rally we did at the capital demanding prison reform when our son Freedom called. In 2016, we allowed the twins to leave high school their sophomore year, get their GED, and start college early. Because they had been homeschooled since completing the eighth grade and worked with me at the car dealership I'd opened in New Orleans, we determined they were prepared to test out of high school and pursue their college education sooner. So both Freedom and Justus were in their freshman year at Tulane at sixteen years old. On this particular day, Freedom shared with me that he had just heard a powerful

speaker at Loyola University whose lecture a friend had recommended. Apparently, the man was a prominent political
analyst who had a different perspective on the political process—a subject Freedom was very much interested in. Even
as a young kid, this little boy was entranced by conversations
and books on politics. He was even elected to his first office
at four years old when he became president of the Kiddie
Corner at Angola prison.

Freedom was also calling me about the event because
he was supposed to be helping me at the dealership at the
time. There were a couple of cars that needed to go to the
mechanic.

"Hey Mama, I just left this lecture with this man Frank
Luntz. And guess what? The governor was in the room
tonight."

"What?" I asked. "The governor was in the room, and
you left the room?!"

"Yeah, you told me you needed me to go fix this car. And
I need to catch the mechanic before he closes."

"No, turn back around and get your butt back to that
engagement."

"Wait! Check this out. Before I left the room, I asked
Frank a question, and he answered. But then he said, 'Hey
kid, what are you doing here at seventeen years old and in
a suit this time of night? I don't even wear a suit.' Mama, I
told him I was a student at Tulane and guess what he said?"

I waited.

"He said to the president of Loyola, 'Hey, we need to get
this guy a scholarship over here at Loyola!'"

My mind was blown at this point. But Freedom just kept
going.

"Then he said, 'Hey kid, don't leave. I'm going to change your life tonight.'"

I couldn't believe that this boy had left to go get a car fixed after hearing Frank Luntz say that.

"Boy, if you don't get back in that room . . . forget the damn car!"

When Freedom returned to the event, they were closing it out, so he waited in this line with everybody else who wanted to speak to Frank. When Frank appeared, he asked Freedom what his name was.

"Why did your parents give you that name?" he asked after hearing Freedom's answer.

Freedom responded to him sheepishly, "It's a long story."

"Make it short," Frank said.

Freedom shared with him that his parents were incarcerated and had decided to name their twins Freedom and Justus. Frank seemed to really respond to the story and turned to introduce Freedom to the governor like they were old friends. Frank then had one of his assistants exchange information with our son, and the next day, Freedom received an email inviting him to brunch the following Saturday because Frank was staying in town for Jazz Fest.

Of course, Freedom said yes, and he came home all excited about their conversation. "Mom, I heard that President Barack Obama once said that when Frank Luntz invites you to dinner, you go!"

"Well, Freedom, I guess you got your answer as to whether or not you need to meet him for coffee."

After helping Freedom get ready for and head off to his meeting, I left to go work on one of the vehicles. Yes, I know how to change brakes and engine oil too.

And as soon as I got on the road, Freedom called and said, "Hey, Mr. Luntz wants to know if you want to join us for breakfast."

"Listen, I wouldn't dare turn down a breakfast invitation from Mr. Luntz, but it's going to take me a minute to get there because I have got to get dressed. I can't go to meet the man in my car mechanic clothes."

So I went back home and put myself together. I threw on one of my big Southern belle hats and walked through the doors of the Omni Hotel in New Orleans's famed French Quarter with my pearls—a signature for me by now—and a silk dress. Before I sat down, I caught the twinkle in Freedom's eyes letting me know I nailed it. My boy was impressed with his mama's impromptu appearance.

Frank's first question to me was a doozy. "How do you get a child to be like this? I deal with a lot of children who are underprivileged or going through hardships. I've never seen a child this mature and brilliant beyond his years. From what he tells me, he has brothers who he says are better than he is. How does this happen? How is this kid not angry? Why is he not mad? Why hasn't he dropped out of school?"

As flustered on the inside as I was at the flurry of questions, I knew the answer. "Well, Mr. Luntz," I said, "it's just love. Love is the most divine chemical in the universe."

It may not be the truth many expect. Not one bit. But I bear witness that love dissolves everything that is not of itself. I told Frank that day that, while we may be an incarcerated family, we're still a family who loves one another very deeply and will go to the ends of the earth for each other. Even prison walls couldn't stop that.

"With love," I said, "all things are possible. Yes, even

enduring two decades in some of the most savage conditions known to humankind."

I'd already told Freedom before he left to meet with Frank
to really think about how this gentleman could assist him in
life. So, Freedom knew exactly what he wanted.

Sitting in front of Mr. Luntz, Freedom's requests were
specific and urgent.

"How can I help you?" Frank asked Freedom.

"Mr. Luntz, I need my daddy home. Not for me, but for
my baby brother, because he deserves to grow up with our
pops."

"The governor was in the room that night. Why didn't
you say something?" Frank asked.

"Mr. Luntz, come on now. Really? What was I going to
say? 'Hey, Governor, my dad's locked up. You think you can
help?'"

I understood how Freedom was feeling. Unfortunately,
there has always been too much embarrassment that goes
on around these subject matters. Many children, even my
own sometimes, don't feel like they have the liberty to speak
freely about their experiences in those spaces.

"You're right," Frank said. "I generally don't ever ask for
anything, but I have a meeting set with your governor soon.
When I meet with him, I'm going to bring your family to
his attention."

Freedom wasn't done though. There was more he wanted.
He asked for help with getting the 20/45 geriatric parole bill
passed because it wasn't just our family who needed help.
He also shared with Frank that he was hopeful for some
scholarship money for school.

Frank wasted no time on that last thing. He immediately

called the president of Loyola right there while we were at the table. He found a merit-based scholarship for Freedom that covered most, but not all, of Freedom's tuition. He would still need $9,000. Mr. Luntz then said to me, "Hey, I realize this doesn't cover all of his tuition. I'm going to write a check for $7,000, at least for that first semester. You'll have to figure it out from there."

I'm Sibil Fox Richardson. That wasn't going to be a problem. I would do what I had to do, like I've always done.

As for the $2,000 difference, it just so happened that Freedom had a Coogan account from when he acted in a commercial for the unveiling of the Martin Luther King statue in Washington, DC. Freedom was the principal actor in that commercial when he was eleven years old. On October 16, he would be turning eighteen and could access the money. Guess how much money he had in his Coogan account?

Exactly $2,000.

It was enough to pay the remaining portion of his first semester at Loyola University, where Freedom would go on to serve as a resident hall advisor, senator, vice president, and president in the Student Government Association (SGA), and become a member of Alpha Phi Alpha Fraternity, Inc.

Freedom passed his first piece of legislation at Loyola as SGA president. He implemented a policy change that added a voting student member to the governing board of Loyola University. The first voting student seat on the board of any Jesuit university. Our boy was building his legacy.

Frank's offer to speak with the governor was another ball of wax. It was so interesting to me, because I had been on this journey for twenty years, and only one other person had ever offered to help us. That was Pastor McClain, who had offered to go and speak to the district attorney Bob Levy on our behalf in the early days of our appeal process. But sure enough, three weeks later, Frank called again. He said he just happened to be in town, even though I would later learn that it was only the second time in over a decade that he had been to New Orleans back-to-back in one year. This time he wanted to meet with the other boys because Freedom had told him that they were more impressive than Freedom was. He invited us to dinner at the ultra-fancy Windsor Court Hotel. However, the boys' palates were not quite as receptive to the menu, for which Frank quickly recognized and apologized.

But while there, he kept asking the boys questions about their lives. By that time, Remington was in dental school at Meharry College, Lawrence was in college at Southern University, Freedom and Justus were both freshmen at Tulane, and little Robert was in homeschool and was street performing.

"Wow!" Frank said. "I have never seen anything like this in my life. Your family is very impressive. Your son Freedom is the most impressive person I've met in the past twenty-five years. And I don't say anything that I don't mean."

We were all so honored. As soon as dinner was over, Rob called, and Mr. Luntz spoke with him on the phone.

ROB

When I talked to Frank, naturally I had my reservations. But his voice was calm and his words were steady and well chosen. He told me what he was capable of but made me no promises other than the fact that he would present our family's matter to the governor. That was everything I needed to know. I was elated that Frank was willing to help. I briefly explained the particulars of my case and then thanked Frank for his intervention. Something about the moment reminded me of the biblical tale of Joseph who told the cupbearer, "Remember me when it is well with you" (Gen. 40:14 NKJV). Frank was not being pardoned like the cupbearer, but he *was* scheduled to meet with our governor in the coming days.

I felt good about my conversation with Frank. It's one thing to have someone with a compassionate heart, but it's another thing altogether to have somebody with able hands.

When the conversation came to a close, Frank asked, "Is there anything further?"

To which I responded, "Whenever it's good for you, I simply ask that you let the king know that I am here."

FOX

It was just one of those opportunities where we knew God was working, but we couldn't see how it was going to pan out. At the very least, our boy would have a mentor who could help him grow in his chosen field. But I could sense there was something else. I knew that I was in the presence of someone who could make things happen.

Frank's able hands would be very much in use on June 9, 2017, when he had his meeting with the governor. As God would have it, I was on my way to Angola that same day. I didn't know what time the meeting was happening, but I prayed my heart out about it. *God, you ain't brought us this far to leave us here.* At about 10:00 a.m., as I was on the road, my phone rang. It was Frank Luntz.

243

"I just met with your governor, and he has given me his word that if you all make it past his pardon board, he will sign your clemency."

My heart swelled! That was all we needed to hear. Not only did we have an opportunity with 20/45, but now we also had the possibility of clemency as another road home.

ROB

On my end, I was walking on eggshells at Angola. I didn't want any trouble. If I had received a write-up of any kind during that time period, my pardon process would have been null and void. Anything could have set me backward. Something as simple as leaving my towel on the bed could have gotten me a write-up. Or having too many shoes out and not stored the proper way. It was all stupid stuff, but any of it could automatically revoke my pardon opportunity. So imagine me, tiptoeing around prison for ten months, trying to conduct myself in a way that I would stay clear of anything that even looked like trouble.

It was all on the line.

But I was inspired by the challenge nonetheless. The idea of having two possibilities for release lined up—the 20/45 geriatric parole release and a commitment for the governor's signature upon a successful recommendation for clemency by the board—gave me more vigor and zeal as I moved through the prison. No one knew what I had going on, so it was like a quiet song I was singing in my own heart. But I did know that the men around me noticed the fire that had been lit in my spirit. And maybe they, too, were motivated by the way I was carrying myself.

FOX AND ROB

For the first time in decades, we were actually at a place where we could start imagining a shared future together. We had long ago found our way back to each other, and everything felt right. Now it was time to make our *re*-union right in the eyes of God. By 2017, we'd talked at length about re-marrying, but Rob had been adamant for years at that point that he didn't want to remarry while we were still in prison. With everything seeming to come together, we didn't think that it would be long before Rob would be released, and then we'd have a glorious wedding at home. On the other hand, we realized a significant amount of time had passed, and we both were very eager to restore our marriage. Especially when you consider the fact that, aside from our paperwork, nothing about our commitment to one another had ever changed.

It was final. We were getting remarried. This thirty-year love project was unstoppable. The bars of Angola be damned.

FOX

A woman I'd met who'd been visiting her husband in Angola told me how she'd gone about getting married without requesting permission from the prison. The only thing we needed to do was have Rob sign a notarized letter for us to get our marriage license. And then we could take that to whoever was marrying us, as long as they were registered as a marriage officiant of the city, and they would perform the ceremony.

ROB

This way, we were able to bypass the system that Angola had in place. They'd created their own policies for people to be married and have the facility's chaplain officiate it. The problem is that they treated people who got married in prison with such disregard. They would send them jumping through hoops with all these rigorous forms, classes, and processes. Once again, it felt dehumanizing. I felt like I shouldn't have to have someone's permission to put my family back together on paper.

I do think that there were other reasons it took me so long to agree to remarry Fox while I was still locked up. A part of me was holding on to the hurt and pain I had experienced during our divorce. I'd grown comfortable with keeping our relationship open-ended because it felt safer that way. I didn't have to consider losing our relationship if she chose to move on again. But by then I'd also gone through several semesters of seminary training and a myriad of classes on marriage and family. I was a different person.

At the end of the day, I understood that my love for her was bigger than my own apprehensions. And our love was bigger than even our own individual flaws. In our first go-around, we didn't really have a vision for our marriage. We had dreams but no mission. This time around, we had dreams *and* a vision we were building.

FOX AND ROB

The first time around, we got married out of love, out of the emotions of our hearts. There was a level of foolish naivete.

246

But we had lived a bit since then. We weren't just guided by our emotions anymore. This second time around, we allowed our minds and souls to enter the mix. There was a higher level of processing that was reflective of the maturity we'd both reached. We had a better command of our expectations and what we were both willing to contribute to and be hopeful for in our marriage.

FOX

So I found a minister to marry us. We brought the notarized paperwork to Sula Spirit, the prayer warrior who'd once prayed over me when I was facing the roughest part of this journey post-release. She was the person I wanted to reunite us. Then we set a date for our wedding.

November 13, 2017.

The same date that Rob and I had met thirty years prior.

On that day, four of our sons—Lawrence, Freedom, Justus, and little Robert—and I made our way over to Sula's Temple, a quaint space that had an altar in it. It looked like a utility shed in a backyard from the outside, but Sula had transformed it into a magical, sacred space. There were lit candles and the sound of rhythmic drumming. We removed our shoes and paid tribute to our ancestors, a common tradition in African and African American culture. The elders are our great cloud of witnesses (see Heb. 12:1) and the people of faith who ran their race before us. Sula stood over me and prayed for our marriage in Rob's absence. Then Rob called, and by a beautifully lit moon, with our boys present, we, once again, committed to one another legally and in the eyes of God.

At that moment, we felt like we had the final piece to put our family back together. What God had brought together, let no man put asunder (see Matt. 19:6). Let no injustice, no prison walls, and no aggressive state sanctions separate what God had brought together. We were now one step closer to holding each other in our arms. It was about restoration. The whole roller coaster of our journey together had been about exactly that. Everything that we had been fighting for, God was about to grant us.

ROB

I was so excited that night. From the other end of the phone, I closed my eyes and imagined what the space and temple might look like. I also held an image of Fox and the boys in my mind, and I was overwhelmed with the beauty of what we'd birthed into this world. It was flawed, for sure. But it was magnificent in every way. When I opened up my eyes, I stared out of the dorm window into the starlit night. So much had been taken from us. But with this act of faith, we were on the brink of everything being returned. Freedom hovered so close.

When Ron came to the prison to visit me, I really thought he was coming to celebrate.

"I don't have good news, man."

Denied.

We really thought the outcome was going to be different. Had we underestimated the insidiousness of the system that much? Commissioner Robinson had recommended that our application for relief under 20/45 be granted. She believed in us, in our humanity as a family who deserved a second chance. But she wasn't the final say.

We'd heard that Robinson had been pressured internally to change her ruling, citing that this would open a floodgate of reopened cases like mine that no one wanted. And it would have. That's what we were hoping for. We wanted to bring relief not only to our own family, including our nephew Ontario who was still imprisoned, but also to the families who'd poured money into helping Rob make this argument before the court—*and* the four hundred to six hundred families impacted by this reinterpretation, people who could have their family members returned home. This was going to be a victory for all of us.

Of course, they couldn't have that. Too many bodies—and money—lost.

It was devastating to hear that the judge had trumped Commissioner Robinson's recommendation and ordered her to rewrite it. But I chose to not let that pain penetrate me. I'd been here before. People had been telling me no, denying me, all my life. And I always found another way.

FOX AND ROB

Two and a half years after the initial application for civil action of Rob's sentence under 20/45, it was all over. Or so *they* thought. We were so wired after that denial. It wasn't desperation at this point. It was conviction. We knew that God doesn't close one door without opening another one. The tunnel might be a little longer than we thought, but there was still light. We had a signature on lock. Not too long after Ron's unsettling visit, we got a message: our hearing before the pardon board was set for May 14, 2018.

15

VICTORY IS MINE

Power concedes nothing without a demand.

Frederick Douglass, from an address
on West India Emancipation

ROB

Imagine working every day, morning to night, for years on something that you know you qualify for, know you are the best candidate for, and all that work means nothing in the end. That can create a bruise on your heart. We were devastated with the outcome of the 20/45 petition.

But we also were not going to be denied. Again, we chose to trust God, which meant trusting the process, even if our reality was not yet reflecting our beliefs. God is omnipotent, omniscient, and omnipresent. God can do whatever God wants. God is not subject to physical limitations like man. God is all-knowing. He is aware of the past, present, and future. God is all-present, capable of being everywhere at the same time. And this pardon hearing was no exception. God's power is infinite.

Ron Haley felt so bad about what happened with the 20/45 application denial that he agreed to represent us pro bono before the pardon and parole board alongside Jim Craig. Jim, executive director for the Roderick and Solange MacArthur Justice Center, represented some of the most important cases regarding police brutality in Louisiana and Mississippi. Although he had never handled a pardon proceeding before, he was always up for a good fight. And he, too, was offering his services pro bono. After submitting a successful application to the Louisiana Board of Pardon and Parole, we were headed into our hearing.

When May 14 came around—which was also my son Mahlik's birthday—I was beyond excited. We'd built what I believed was a solid strategy for approaching the board. The board consisted of five members appointed by the governor to review and take action on pardon and commutation of sentence applications. Upon a favorable recommendation from the board, an applicant's request is then forwarded to the governor for signature. This is a discretionary step but must happen in order for the recommendation of the board to be executed. Thank God for angels like Frank Luntz.

There were many days when our sessions were like a war room. Fox, Ron, and Jim all sitting around a table with me on the phone, walking through every scenario, every word that may or may not be said. We were able to salvage so much of the information gathered from our previous losses and incorporate them into our presentation before the pardon board. This was my last remaining opportunity for freedom.

Our strategy started with the seemingly simple: what I was going to wear. I went around the prison and borrowed everything from dress shoes to a designer pair of jeans. A crisp white shirt completed the look along with a tie that had been brought in by Attorney Haley. Little did I know Haley had taken it a step further and brought me an entire suit to wear. How he got through the front gate with it, I still don't know. But what I did know is that I was not about to put that suit on. I had gotten approval from the warden to wear the tie but did not have approval for a suit. Everything was riding on this day. I wasn't about to risk losing this opportunity all because I wasn't wearing a prison uniform or approved clothing. Plus, I knew they didn't want me looking too much like the gentleman or the human I was.

Another consideration we needed to make was how many light-skinned or white people were going to be with me at Angola, because Fox had recently discovered that, due to poor technology, dark-skinned people unfortunately didn't show up clearly on the screens where the Pardon Board would be watching from Baton Rouge.

Additionally, we thought about who would be at the prison by my side and who would be with Fox as part of our support in Baton Rouge. They'd recently changed the rules so that the person who was up for pardon, or clemency, would not be allowed to appear in person, but via video. So we had to consider how to divide and conquer.

Our planning was *that* intricate and intense.

One of the final pieces of our strategy was selecting those

who would speak on my behalf. First on the list was Warden Kevin Benjamin, the same person who offered me my very first job when I arrived at Angola in 1999, as well as the person who got me out of isolation and back to the main prison in 2011. I guess you might say even in hell, God provides an angel. Because we wanted to make sure that we put our children in front of them, the boys were going to be present in Baton Rouge. That said, we decided to not allow any of them to speak. We didn't want to subject them to some of the heartless and brutal treatment we'd witnessed with others who'd gone before the board. I wanted to minimize as much of that as I could for my family.

FOX

Exactly. Being formerly incarcerated myself and a codefendant on this offense, I also elected not to speak. In preparation for Rob's hearing, I'd started sitting in as a member of the public to watch the board hearings. I saw firsthand how callously they could treat some family members who came up to speak on behalf of their loved ones. I didn't see a need to put myself in the hot seat and let them humiliate me in front of our children for the choices I'd made in the past. I wanted all the good that Rob and I had done since then to take center stage instead.

ROB

Fox not speaking actually worked in our favor because it didn't give them an opportunity to rip us apart. They couldn't try us all over again. Plus, we felt that some members of the greater community who knew us would be better to speak on our family's behalf and on my rehabilitation and potential contribution to society.

One of the first people we enlisted for help was Skip Casey. That was definitely a strategic move, as he was a white man and a staunch Republican from Monroe whose house and grounds Fox used to clean while she was in the halfway house there.

Skip was a devout Christian man and had become a pen pal to me during my time in Camp J segregated lockdown. We'd butt heads sometimes because I was always going to respect other people's religious practices without judgment or hope of conversion, and he didn't understand that. But the one thing we emphatically agreed upon was that God is love. Our thinking was that, because Skip had gotten to know Fox and me at our lowest moment, he would be an ideal reflection of the greater community's perception of us then and now.

There was some rejection during this planning time though. People we thought would gladly speak on my behalf let us down in the end. Norris Henderson, a renowned formerly incarcerated-person-turned-activist and friend of the board, told us that he would speak at the hearing. We saw him at visitation on Sunday, the day before the hearing. Monday came and we called him repeatedly, asking when he would arrive. There was no response. No return phone call. He didn't even bother to show up.

Honestly, that hurt. We'd been weighing a big portion of our testimonies on him. My thinking was that we had been imprisoned together for years, and even upon his release, Fox continued to foster the relationship around criminal justice reform measures. He'd been around me long enough to weigh in on my character and speak to my rehabilitation efforts. We were hopeful to borrow from his social equity among members of the board and thought his presence would have served as icing on the cake.

Nevertheless, having two lawyers to represent me and speak on behalf of the family felt necessary. We figured one would work as a cleanup person. He would sit back, analyze how the proceedings were progressing, and make the closing statements. The other would focus on the opening statements. The idea that we could have two committed and capable attorneys working fervently on our behalf felt like such a huge blessing when I thought about all those years of scrounging up money and selling cars to get money up for representation. And now, there were two, and both were offering pro bono representation!

All in all, we had fifty people ready to show up in Baton Rouge. But apparently, that was too much support. They told us we had to choose thirteen people. So, Fox and the five oldest boys went to Baton Rouge to be in front of the Pardon Board. Little Robert came to Angola. Ms. Peggy, Fox's mother, and Ms. Peggy's brother came to Angola to show solidarity with the family dynamic. In fact, she was the only living parent between the both of us.

So, by the time May 14 rolled around, we were ready. This felt like the biggest moment of our lives, and everything had to be done perfectly. There could be no mistakes.

FOX

The morning of May 14, Laurita Barras Dollis, one of the queens of the Black Masking Indians of New Orleans and a friend of mine, gathered some other queens and spiritual leaders on the phone, and they prayed down heaven over us on our way to the hearing. That meant so much to me. It was probably the first time someone in the community had said to me, "I want to put together a prayer call for you and your family." And not only did she get up early that morning for the prayer call but she went to Angola to be with my husband that day.

After we finished prayer, Rob called us as we were making our way to Baton Rouge in the car. "Did you talk to State Representative Katrina Jackson?" he asked as we went up and down our checklist.

"I did."

I didn't have a deep, long-standing relationship with Katrina. However, we did share a godmother in Monroe. When I was at the halfway house, I'd self-appointed Esther Gallow, one of the leaders in that community, as my godmother because she'd believed in me and hired me to be the Director of Public Relations for her nonprofit, Booker T. Community Outreach. Katrina was a young lady who also considered Esther her community mother, as Esther was integral in helping Katrina get elected.

Back in April 2018, I was at the capitol trying to get some bills passed at the state legislature that would ensure that a person in Louisiana couldn't get more time for armed robbery than someone who was convicted of manslaughter. The bill never made it out of committee, and that was devastating. It felt like the simplest of corrections the state legislature could have done. There was no way a person who committed armed robbery should have more time than someone who'd taken a life. But they refused to see the moral error in the law. I was livid and hanging on by a string in the hallway where the committee met when I ran into Katrina Jackson.

"What's going on?" she said.

"I can't believe these people. I just cannot believe the evil that exists in this space! People are just not wanting to do the right thing for no reason," I ranted.

I normally never let people see me out of order, but she'd caught me at a hard time. With tears in my eyes, I began to explain to her about the bill and Rob's upcoming pardon hearing.

"This is the last opportunity I have to put my family together, and nobody sees this as wrong."

After some consolation, Katrina and I parted ways. Her last words to me were, "Well, just give me a call."

So when Rob called that morning of the hearing and reminded me about her, I decided as a last-ditch effort to reach out. I was pulling out all the stops. I called her the morning of to see if she could come speak, or at the very least write a favorable letter. She chose the latter, and I was grateful. But then something changed in her voice.

"You know what?" she said. "I'm in Monroe, but I'm going to get up, throw myself together, and put on a skirt. Let me get on this road."

Wow! Look at God!

Monroe was about a three-and-a-half-hour trip, and she hadn't even gotten dressed yet. But she was coming.

ROB

That was a big deal. We even heard that the board gave her a legislative courtesy—something that could only be extended to elected officials—and waited for her to arrive. All because she wanted to speak. Unbeknownst to us, she had personally called ahead to let the board know that she wanted to speak on our family's behalf and asked them to give her time to make it.

But they didn't tell *us* that.

An hour away from the live hearing in Angola, I sat with my people in the visitation shed of the prison, waiting to hear my name called to go before the board. And, sure enough, my name was called first. We gathered in a circle and were led in prayer by Reginald Watts, a fellow incarcerated Bible College alumnus who I'd asked to bless us before we entered the room. About twenty-five of our faithful supporters, Ron, and I headed into the room where the hearing was being held. Almost immediately, the cameras were turned off and everything shut down. Next, I heard an authoritative voice say, "Hold up. They are not going to take you right now. Go back out."

It was nerve-racking. *What in the world is going on?*

First, Ron thought that maybe they made a mistake, and we weren't going to go first. This would have been great because it gave us time to warm up and maybe even do some quick sparring. But then an hour passed, and we were on pins and needles.

"Something is wrong," Ron said.

Ron went up front to see if he could get a phone call and figure out why we were delayed. He wanted to reach out to Jim, the other attorney in Baton Rouge, to find out what the issue was, but he couldn't get a phone call out. So we sat longer, thinking things through. And the longer we sat, the more worried I became.

258

FOX

That's because all hell had broken loose. It felt like the moment we had been waiting for our whole lives was about to be snatched away from us in an instant.

At this time, we were filming the documentary *Time* that went on to be released on Amazon Prime and nominated for an Academy Award. The film crew was present at the hearing, although they were under specific instruction from me to not bring their cameras out until the hearing was over. Two years prior, Rob was concerned that if we did not put a spotlight on our story and the injustice associated with it, we might never get free. He then suggested we do a documentary to chronicle everything that had happened so far and raise awareness about our matter. So I began working to make it happen. And in a moment of divine intervention, we received a call from director Garrett Bradley, who was in the midst of making a short doc. She reached out to Gina Womack, executive director at the Family and Friends of Louisiana's Incarcerated Children organization (FFLIC), looking for someone to interview for her original short doc *Alone*, funded by the *New York Times*. I agreed to participate and, after completing the interviews for the project, asked Garrett if she would go back and pitch our story to the *Times* team to see if they'd be interested in telling our family's story. They agreed, and the rest would become history. We were so excited. Now, more people would know about our family's plight!

However, prior to the hearing, I had made it very clear to those filming the documentary not to bring the cameras out until the proceedings were over and we had left the premises.

259

One thing I have learned is that nothing infuriates the government like cameras! Unfortunately, an overzealous cameraman decided to pull out his camera and stand right at the front door of the pardon building. This sent everyone into a frenzy. The head of public relations for the Department of Corrections came out with security officers to investigate. Security was heightened. They all wanted to know what the hell was going on.

Our film producer spoke to the officials without speaking to me first, identifying herself as a filmmaker working with the *New York Times*. For obvious reasons, I had not told them about the documentary we were filming. The film producer had been invited to the hearing as a spectator only so she could gain greater insight into what the hearing proceedings were like for future narration. Certainly not to document the proceedings. This revelation almost cost us our hearing. I was shaken. All I could think about was how a simple social media post sent Rob to isolation for nine months. What would happen when they discovered a film crew?

We believe that the only thing that saved us in that moment was the fact that Representative Katrina Jackson was coming to speak on behalf of our family. The board had already given her legislative courtesy and were now obligated to wait until she showed up. If that were not the case, they probably would have pulled our hearing. We would've lost it all behind a documentary that we were hoping would bring greater awareness to our matter. Instead, it nearly cost us our last shot at freedom.

My heart was broken. When I discovered they had busted the cinematographer who had set up outside filming, everything in me shook with fear. There I was, standing in the middle of the room, with a group of people there to support my husband and me, and all I could do was lower my head as tears streamed down my face. At that moment, I connected with my ancestors. I understood why, when in the most excruciating pain, they would have to sing. At that moment, I could do nothing but sing. I started slow and deep. "Victory is mine. I told Satan to get thee behind."[1]

Then I sang it louder. And louder. Then the people in that room started singing with me. On that day, with God having gone before me, setting a table in the presence of our enemies, I was not going to be denied. On that day, all that we had worked for, all that we had sacrificed, was not going to be swept away from us because of one woefully out of line videographer.

ROB

I learned all of what happened later, and I'm so glad I did. I'm grateful that Ron could not get a phone call out of the prison to find out what was actually going on in Baton Rouge, because I know that I would have been mentally shattered. My calm and peace would have been ripped away from me. Especially when I knew that we'd done everything right. We'd dotted all the i's and crossed all the t's. If we were going to be denied that day, it could not be at our own hands. It wasn't going to be because we weren't prepared. We had the right responses to all of the questions. We had the right people in position and places to speak. Everything, we thought, was perfect.

By the grace of God, the hearing was not pulled. Katrina made it there, and they finally let us all know—the Baton Rouge and Angola contingents—that we were coming up next to be heard.

Representative Katrina Jackson took the floor first, and she held the board—some of whom she'd known her whole career—in rapt attention:

> I've seen a number of cases where the sentence did not fit the crime. And one thing I promised my district was when there were opportunities, whether it be a family member or not, where I could advocate on someone's behalf that was truly reformed and that I could seek the true purpose of the criminal justice system, that I would; and that's why I'm here today.
>
> I take it very seriously, when it comes to my capacity as an attorney, to ask you to please review someone's case. I want to make sure that it has merit. Every day, we have a chance to legislate in a way that we can touch morality. And one of those areas has been for those who are not incarcerated to be able to take proper care for their children. I am most impressed that Mr. Richardson has been able to do that while incarcerated. He has had such a major impact on these children's lives. Every day as an attorney, I face cases where fathers have not been as involved nor had anywhere the impact on the kids' involvement.
>
> At some point, when individuals have been rehabilitated, I think it's our duty, and your duty as the board, to recognize that. There's nobody here in opposition to him receiving commutation of sentence because they've done all that they could. He's done all that he could. Most inmates don't have the benefit of a supportive family. He has. And then some do, and they never really reform themselves. But he has. He's

taken advantage of everything that the Department of Corrections has offered by way of job training and education.
And that has been most impressive to me as well.

The original sentence that was offered to him on the pleas
was one that, to me, was fair; however, through bad advice,
he selected not to take it. And at some point, even when
citizens of this state made the wrong decisions, you don't
continue to punish them for that. I believe at some point,
you really look to see if they have rehabilitated themselves.
If they're ready to enter society, or they have a supportive
system. I can honestly stand here and say this is one person
that has that. And to me that's what matters in our life. I
am in tears speaking for him today, because you get a lot
of highlights in your life. You get a lot of things to do as
a public official and as an attorney, but this is one of those
that are near and dear to my heart. Advocating for those
who deserve a second chance.

As a Christian, I always tell people, and most of the legislative body, that had we gotten caught with some of the
things we did in our teens, we wouldn't be sitting in these
seats today. What I mean by that is no one has ever been im-
mune to doing something that they regret. So the only thing
that separates us today from this inmate, this person that's
asking for leniency and fairness of this board, is that he was
caught in the moment. He's truly paid his debt to society,
and to keep him in jail for another forty years would be a
slap in the face to the criminal justice system.

I wouldn't be before you if I didn't know this family personally. I wouldn't be before you if I truly did not believe in
my heart of hearts that this gentleman was rehabilitated and
ready to reenter society. And I thank you so much for waiting on me. I did not want to miss the opportunity to speak
before you. Some people write letters. But sometimes, when

you have someone that deserves a second chance as much as he does, you want to stand and speak on his behalf. I respect all of you. This is a thankless job, just like ours. I hope that you, as you listen to the testimonies that are before you today, see this as I see it. As a chance for us to issue leniency to someone who truly deserves it.

Representative Jackson also said that she'd never shown up to speak for members of her own family who were incarcerated, but what we'd accomplished as a unit was worth showing up for.

Our spirits soared listening to this woman. She wasn't doing this on the strength of her and Fox's relationship, because they didn't know each other like that. It was like their shared godmother, who'd just passed only three months before, had orchestrated it all from heaven. God and Esther Gallow were putting in work.

Representative Jackson set the tone for the day. Ron and Jim followed with additional support. We mistakenly thought that having white men speak on our behalf to a predominately white male board would put us over the top, but we now know that wasn't the case. Ironically, they gave Representative Jackson all the respect in the world and chewed out Skip Casey, the conservative, right-aligned, Trump-supporting white male in the room.

One of the board members said, "Well, I don't want to hear from all these people. I want to hear from somebody in the family."

This was uncomfortable for us, because we'd seen how they treated people on the stand, and we wanted to protect our family from this.

"Well, Mr. Richardson—is it *Mr.* Richardson?—who do you want to speak for you from your family?"

The room fell silent as a graveyard. Then, the loudest whispers I'd ever heard grew. In this quaint little room, there were about twenty-five people total who were there in support of us.

Who is it going to be?

It was getting down to the closing parts of the hearing, and when the board members realized that none of the family was going to speak, they started making demands.

"We'd like to hear from the family."

"Let Remington speak," I heard my brother and sister-in-law Ellis and Diane whisper.

In my own mind, I had already reached that conclusion. If anyone was going to speak for me, it would be our son Remington. I knew the level of respect and regard he held for me. And it was only second to his mother.

I proudly responded, "I'd like my son Remington to speak for me."

When Remington took the floor, you could hear a pin drop.

"I've had three graduations in my life," Remington said. "High school. Bachelor's degree. And a master's degree. And none of them, my father was able to attend. Not because he's some kind of deadbeat dad. He's by far not that. He has been present for me and my brothers in every way possible. Only because of the condition he finds himself. A condition that has impacted all of us greatly. But I'll be damned if my dad is not going to be there when I graduate from dental school. So I'm asking y'all with whatever it is that you got in your power to do today, to use that power to grant my father, our family, relief from this situation. There might be a lot of things we deserve, but this ain't one of them. This ain't one of 'em."

You could feel the shift in the room. We even felt it two hours away in Angola. There wasn't a dry eye in the place. After Remi spoke, the board members went into a huddle to make their decision. The screen went blank. When the screen came back on, they rendered their findings.

"We've never heard such conviction and passion in support of a person," was their opening line. Each person on the board had a vote and had to announce their decision. I needed four out of the five votes.

"I am moving to grant immediate parole eligibility in your case, Mr. Richardson," said board member Kenneth Loftin.

One vote.

The second person, Jim Wise, echoed the same sentiments as Loftin.

Two votes.

The third person, Sheryl Ranatza, followed suit.

Three votes.

My heart was racing. Tears welled in the back of my eyes.

The fourth person, Alvin Roche', spoke for a long time. He stated that his decision was based on the exceptional achievements of the children, comments from the warden, and the heartfelt words of Representative Katrina Jackson. It felt like that part in a movie when the music score has risen to a fevered pitch, and everyone is hanging on for dear life, waiting to see what happens next.

"I am moved to side with the others in saying that Mr. Richardson should be granted immediate parole eligibility."

I breathed a huge sigh of relief. I allowed twenty-one years of emotion to crack the surface. But we still needed to hear from the fifth person, Judge Kuhn, a former Louisiana circuit court judge. After retiring, he took on a job as a member of the pardon and parole board, which was considered problematic considering that many of the people coming to the board had already stood before him in their criminal appeals. Let's just say his response was very different from the other members of the board. In his moment of personal privilege, he took the opportunity to tear me completely apart:

> I don't care what deal was offered to you.
>
> I want to tell you something . . . I'm not saying a thing about your family; I'm saying something about you! For you encouraging or allowing what I sat through today.
>
> I have a personal grind here, and that's why I recuse myself. I am number eight of nine kids. My mother had a third-grade education. My daddy was an alcoholic . . . so she raised all of us. I put myself through law school.

He went on to discuss what he and his siblings accomplished despite his background.

> That's their accomplishment. Not yours. It belongs to them. Shame on you for taking the least bit of credit for what they accomplished. Or what your wife accomplished.
>
> This isn't a vehicle to make money. To write books or articles. It's trying to help people in prison. What you've done here today, this dog and pony show, damages that.
>
> I'm so mad, I can hardly think or talk. I don't want a response.
>
> I will never sit on anything involving you.

Even now, it's so hard to share how I was feeling at that

moment. Clearly, this man was triggered. His own trauma was coming to the surface, and he was projecting it my way. But he was tap-dancing on my own insecurities. I had been locked up for over twenty years. Did he not think that I'd wrestled with what that meant to my children every single day I was behind bars?

"Thank you, sir," I responded. What else could I have said?

I'll never forget those awful words. My life hinged on them.

FOX AND ROB

Yes, we did have the votes. But we learned later that the payback they rendered for us filming the documentary was, instead of commuting Rob's sentence to twenty-one years and giving him credit for time served, they'd simply accelerated his parole. This meant that, even though he'd get out of prison, *he'd still have the remaining forty years of his sentence to serve on parole.*

Now that the hearing was over, we were left trying to figure out what it all meant. The pardon board and the parole board were made up of the same people. He'd gone before the pardon board, so did that mean he'd have to go before the same people again for parole? It was so strange and redundant. And nobody seemed to have any answers.

FOX

When they made the announcement that we had the four votes we needed, I did not allow anybody to cheer. I made everyone clear out of there as fast as possible. We couldn't rejoice. It had been too heinous, too horrendous of an experience. The energy was so thick with resentment, and if I'm honest, I was angry. How could they do this to us? We gave the documentary producers an opportunity to tell our story; how dare they violate my trust and start filming at the hearing?

ROB

We didn't want this win to be stolen from us. We were celebrating at Angola, because we didn't know all the ins and outs of what was happening on the other side in Baton Rouge. Yes, Judge Kuhn's words hurt, but we still got it done. We didn't know what *immediate parole eligibility* looked like, but we knew it meant that we were moving in the right direction right now. So, yes, there were tears of joy. Especially from little Robert, who was now twelve years old and right there by my side. It was a powerful moment.

"Dad, does this mean you are coming home?"

"Yes, son. It means exactly that. It means I'm coming home to you, man. I told you I'd make it there."

He smiled that boyish smile of his, and my heart burst.

When the governor first came into office, he'd pardoned sixteen people right off the bat. That news traveled like wildfire throughout the prison. But then there was a pause in that process. By June, there hadn't been any pardons granted. So when I walked back to my dorm that day, back into prison population, there were so many men yelling and beating the windows in celebration. There were fists in the air. It wasn't just my victory. It wasn't just my family's victory. It was every incarcerated person in Angola's victory too. It meant that pardons were possible again. It gave everyone hope.

The recommendation was done. We just needed the governor's signature. How soon would this happen? We didn't know. Under the new governor, they could not pass the state's budget. There was an impasse between parties. That was scary for us. We knew that if he was trying to get his budget passed, we were not going to be a priority. Our state was in disarray and needed funding badly. So the signing of my pardon would have to wait. For how long, we didn't know. Would Governor Edwards renege on his word?

One sweltering day in June, I remember them calling me out of the dorm to let me know that the wardens wanted to see me. *What is this all about?* I was worried, and rightfully so. Getting called for a special meeting with the warden was usually a bad sign. But it wasn't bad at all. They were just letting me know that my pardon had been granted, and I would be hearing from the governor's office in the coming days.

True to his word, on June 26, 2018, after not one or two but three extraordinary legislative sessions had come to a close, Governor Edwards affixed his signature to the pardon board's recommendation of immediate parole eligibility for Robert Glen Richardson, DOC number 3-8-7-4-1-3. The final hearing for release was set for September 13.

FOX

Three months!

They wanted us to wait an additional three months?! You'd think that with the signature of the governor, everything would be all set. That they would simply stamp the documents with a gold seal and send it to the prison. But no, there was always another hoop to jump through.

ROB

I never realized the magnitude of the weight I was carrying until that very moment. The relief was beyond anything I'd felt before. I mean, I wasn't going home that day or the next day, but I was going. This sent ripples through the prison.

"Man, Rob is going home, y'all."

"Congrats, brother!"

"That's so good, yo!"

From the cell blocks to the main prison, everyone had something to say.

A couple of days afterward, the guards called me for mail, and I saw the official documentation in an envelope that, of course, had already been opened. Sergeant Augustine, a male security guard who had spent thirty years working the penitentiary mail room, looked at me and said in his country twang, "It's a pardon! Man, I ain't never seen a gold seal. Been here for thirty years and ain't never seen one of these." Then he slammed the window shut. I could hear him talking on the other side though. "Ain't never seen nothing like this in all this time."

The back door opened, and he came walking out of the mail room. He was holding my pardon paperwork in his hand and showing the other officers. "This one here is on the way home! We got a free man in our midst."

As strange, and maybe embarrassing, as it was to hear him make a fuss, I felt good inside. Because everyone he spoke to seemed genuinely happy for me. Many of them wanted to see the seal with its raised lettering and the state of Louisiana bird, the brown pelican, imprinted on it. The words *union*, *justice*, and *confidence* circled the image. The men who were closest to me wanted to touch it. They wanted to know what one felt like, what it smelled like.

"That thang smell like gold," one man said. "I spent my whole life robbing jewelry stores, so I know what gold smells like. That there is gold bullion."

On my way back to the dormitory, I ran into a fellow classmate in the Bible College. He'd also gone up before the Pardon Board the same time I had and was waiting for his outcome.

"You just got yours today? I'm going to go down there and check my mail too. They probably sent ours together."

Later that evening, I saw him at chow. I could tell he'd been looking for me because he lived on an opposite yard.

"Man, Rob, I need to holler at you. They must have forgotten mine when they sent yours."

That's when I shared with him the truth. Just because you got the recommendation doesn't mean you automatically get the governor's signature. He had to petition the governor for the actual signature.

"Well, somebody told me that my application was sitting on the governor's desk."

I was shocked. Who would lie to him like that? Especially about something so important, with deadlines attached to it. I had to let him know. "That's not how it works. There are no applications on the governor's desk."

Needless to say, as the days went on, he realized that he needed to find someone to help him get the governor's attention so he could sign off on his petition. This kind of disinformation is why it is important for citizens to be educated about the system.

FOX AND ROB

When September 13 arrived, we were leaving nothing to chance. We were still working with Ron and Jim as our attorneys, only this time we put Ron in front of the board in Baton Rouge and Jim stayed at Angola with Rob. Fox worked day and night trying to gather another group of people to take off work and drive hours away to support us. And our community showed up and showed out. People came from Shreveport and beyond. We did have some concerns about Judge Kuhn, who we'd learned was supposed to sit on the board—despite what he'd said in the previous hearing about recusing himself.

We'd asked Representative Katrina Jackson if she knew anything about whether he would be there, but she didn't. "I encourage you to not worry about it though," she'd said. "Because the governor has granted your immediate parole eligibility, that means, in essence, you have been resentenced. And because you have been resentenced, you are now governed by the new rules of pardon and parole that exist."

She went on to share with us that in an earlier legislative session, they'd made it so an incarcerated person no longer needed a unanimous vote in favor of parole. We only needed a majority vote. So even if Judge Kuhn chose to recuse himself or to take a moment of personal privilege at our parole board hearing, we still had the opportunity to convince the other two. But it was still a murky situation for us. *Do we want to be heard by him again? If he is scheduled to be on our board, what should we do about it, knowing how he treated us the last time?*

We ultimately decided that God hadn't brought us this far to leave us.

Just be still.

We'd done our part. We weren't going to worry about it. Like 2 Corinthians 12:9–10 says:

"My grace is sufficient for you, for my power is made perfect in weakness." Therefore I will boast all the more gladly of my weaknesses, so that the power of Christ may rest upon me. For the sake of Christ, then, I am content with weaknesses, insults, hardships, persecutions, and calamities. For when I am weak, then I am strong. (ESV)

ROB

I wasn't satisfied, but I was content. I wasn't happy about this man being part of this process again, but I chose to trust God. I was going to rest knowing that my family was here with me, and we'd done all that we could do. The boys flew back in town again. Mahlik came in from New Jersey. Remington came home from dental school in Nashville. Lawrence, Freedom, Justus, and little Robert were in New Orleans with Fox, but all of them had left their work or school early to be there. We were going to stand together as a family.

In our obedience to God, in being still, God showed out for us one more time.

One day, while awaiting that final hearing, I was in Angola's law library, and a man came up to me and said, "Hey man, I think they're talking about your case over there."

When I looked across the room, I saw Arthur Carter, a brilliant legal mind I'd debated years ago regarding 20/45. A few partitions away, Keith Jones, the newest parole board member, was speaking to a group of guys about how he ended up being the new pardon board member.

Wait, what?

Mr. Jones was telling them about the gentleman he was replacing on the board. A gentleman by the name of Judge Kuhn. God has such a funny sense of humor. According to rumors, Kuhn was reprimanded for the way he handled a pardon board hearing for a gentleman and his family, where the gentleman's son stood up and spoke in favor of his father.

You could have knocked me sideways! He was talking about me! God was making a way for me all along.

Despite the hardships we'd faced daily, we never doubted God's presence and covering. Like Psalm 46:1 says, "God is our refuge and strength, an ever-present help in trouble." When the courts denied us relief, when financial challenges mounted, when separation threatened to take us under, and when doubt raised its evil head, we found refuge in God's promise.

FOX AND ROB

Sure enough, we went before the board, and Rob's parole was granted. They did add some sanctions which, admittedly, were hard for us to take in at first. He had to do sixteen hours of community service monthly, which was fine because so much of our work around prison reform qualified. But he also had a curfew. Rob couldn't be outside any earlier than six o'clock in the morning, nor later than nine o'clock at night. It reminded us of the sundown laws that were imposed against Black people who were up from slavery during Reconstruction and in the earliest twentieth century. After serving twenty-one years in prison with only one write-up related to information Fox shared on the internet, that felt excessive. It felt like we were going from slavery to sharecropping, where our status had changed but our lives still felt extremely limited. It was freedom with a caveat, an asterisk.

Nevertheless, we were grateful for this part of the journey being over. Seven days later, on September 20, 2018, Rob was released from Angola State Penitentiary. *We would be the only incarcerated family to receive clemency in the state of Louisiana in 2018.*

FOX

Listen, when I woke up that first morning that I thought he would be released, my heart was so full. After twenty-one years apart, I was going to get my baby and bring him home. I wanted to be there first thing, to be the first face he saw when he cracked the line between captivity and liberation.

I am going to sit in front of that prison until he is released.

That was the plan. I laid in the middle of my bed that morning and prayed for a good while. I got up and laid the life-size poster of Rob in the middle of our bed. Then, I spread rose petals all over and topped it off with burning sage and a prayer.

And then I learned it would be another day.

I thought he would have been home by now.

But it was okay. He was still coming home. I slept on the couch the next night because I didn't want to ruin the rose petals, and I didn't have any money to buy more.

"Is this Sibil Richardson?"

I don't even remember what all the lady said, because I tuned her out when I heard the golden words.

"Robert Richardson has been released, and we need to know when you're going to be able to pick him up."

"I'm on my way!"

I tore around my house like a banshee, where I gathered my paperwork and got dressed. I barely bothered to comb my hair. I whispered a prayer that this would be the last night I would sleep alone and grabbed my pearls and hat. I called Garrett, the director of the documentary, and asked her to meet me there. She was already on it.

The day we'd waited an eternity for was finally here!

Then I called my friend Maychelle Cooper-Rodney. Our car, the last car left over from the dealership, was not going to make it to Angola. When Rob made parole, Maychelle had told us that she and her husband, Big O, wanted to bless us with a limousine ride home from the prison.

And sure enough, Rob and I rode back to New Orleans in style. Earlier that morning when I got the call, she picked me up, drove me to the prison, and to my surprise, the limo had beat us there.

When we arrived, the fear was still in my bones. Were they going to change their mind? *Lord, I hope not.* I hadn't seen my husband on the other side of those gates in twenty plus years. Nothing could stop us now, right?

ROB

It was a Tuesday morning.

The sun was bright in the sky.

The birds were singing.

And I had a song in my heart, and it was only getting louder.

That morning, I rose, performed my normal rituals, and unpacked from my locker box a T-shirt I'd had made for this special occasion—the words NEVER GIVE UP screened across the front. These words represented a pact I had made to myself when I first arrived at Angola. Not long after that, I went outside and got in a workout. Along the way, I shared some departing words with men who had become my family, some of whom I had spent decades with. Then I waited for them to call my name.

All I was carrying out of the prison with me was a bag of letters and pictures. I took one last look at the bed where I had slept for years and took a deep breath. Then I dapped up a few brothers, walked out of Walnut-4 dorm and through the West Yard gate toward the main prison control center. On the way out, I could see the look on the men's faces. Some of them were cheering. Others had the same look of utter bewilderment I had twenty years ago when I'd see guys leaving. I used to wonder what it felt like to leave. I wanted to know if I would be so lucky.

When I finally exited the prison annex and got in the van to be driven to the front gate, it was like I could feel God smiling down on me. His redemption. His favor. His joy at our joy. I looked back at all of the pastures that made up the prison. The same places I had worked. The same fields

I imagined that my enslaved African ancestors had worked, trying to find good in something that was spoiled and rotten at its core.

When I finally made it to the Receiving Center, I had a flashback of when I entered the prison for the very first time. It had been over two decades ago, and what used to be the old cells for death row were now being used as housing for women prisoners displaced by the great flood of 2016. It was heart-wrenching. It felt like I was escaping certain death, and I suppose, in many ways I was doing exactly that.

When the gates opened, I saw her. The woman I'd loved for what seemed like an eternity. Fox was screaming and yelling and throwing her fist in the air! There was a guy to my left saying something to me, but his voice faded into the distance as my own inner excitement swelled inside me. Fox's voice overpowered the atmosphere. Her shouts were a fury of joy. The day we had longed for was finally here! It was indeed a dream come true. We embraced, and I could feel the love that radiated from her being; and this time, no one would ever make us let go. This woman had loved me for the better part of both our lives, and I wanted nothing more than to spend the rest of my days loving her.

FOX

At first, I couldn't run. I couldn't shout. I couldn't do anything. I was immobilized. But then it was like the earth shifted when I saw him. Free. Unshackled. Reaching for me! That's when I fell into his arms. All I could do was scream out in victory—today, it was ours!

FOX AND ROB

There was still this anxious feeling in both of us. This sense that maybe it was a dream. We got in that limo and pulled off the prison grounds. That's when it really hit us. It was happening. Rob was free! No more gates or cages. Prison was no longer a part of our lives.

We sat there in a daze for a second. Watching the prison buses heading toward the prison even as we were leaving, heading home. Then we snapped out of it. Almost at the same time, we realized that we were free and could touch each other. We could be a normal husband and wife. We could flirt and make love, and no one could stop us. Our humanity was restored. And so, we acted on that. We reacquainted ourselves with each other, right there in the back of the limousine. Twenty-one years and four days of simmering fire turned into a blaze of love.

The longing that spanned a quarter of a century and swelled our insides came bursting forth that day. It was an indescribable moment, as it is for most incarcerated families. Even though we knew the date and had been working tirelessly toward that day, seeing those gates open with our loved one on the other side was overwhelming. Seeing each other felt like the culmination of all the hope and faith we'd held on to all that time—a massive exhale.

The arrival home was momentous. Everyone was overjoyed. Fox had been intentional about keeping some semblance of Rob's presence in the home, whether that meant speaking his name aloud and often, or the cardboard rendering of him she'd had made years ago—the one everyone called Flat Rob.

But Rob in the flesh was an entirely different feeling for all of us—especially the boys. Remington and Mahlik received the FaceTime call of their dream. Tears poured from Freedom's eyes when we surprised him with Rob at a doctor's office. Little Robert, the only one who'd never known a time when his dad wasn't in jail, held his mouth wide open in surprise as Rob toppled him with kisses outside of his school.

"Man, where you come from?" he joked.

"I've been waiting for this," Rob said as he held his youngest tight. "It's like a dream."

Just like a soldier returning home from war, there is a significant adjustment or reintegration period that formerly incarcerated families must endure and manage post-release. There's a hunger for normality. For the way things were. We had to realize that, in two decades, the world and the way we navigated it had dramatically changed. There was a new normal that required new language and new ways of being. People had also changed. Fox was not the same woman she was when this journey began. Rob was not the same. So we were both learning who we were *to each other* daily. The beauty of this is we still have our past lessons. That hasn't changed. We could carry what we'd learned into this new season of our lives, even as we leave the not-so-great parts of our old selves behind. Post-release, and especially after living through a global pandemic, we now understand more than ever that we are inherently abundant beyond measure. We've got our lives, our health, our strength, our love, and the love of God. That's what matters. We didn't fully grasp that in 1997. And that sent our lives spiraling. We didn't know then what we will never forget now—family is everything, and everything is family.

EPILOGUE

To Be Free Is to Free Others

FOX AND ROB

There are moments that truly feel like a kind of resurrection. Like our lives are so completely different from anything we've ever known before, and it feels, well, surreal. That feeling was at the core of our emotions as we walked the red carpet at the ninety-third annual Academy Awards. Our story—chronicled in the most acclaimed film of 2020, the Amazon Studios Original documentary *Time*—was rightfully being celebrated as one of resilience and radical love in the newly transformed Los Angeles Union Station at the most exclusive Oscars ceremony ever.

As we stood there, the energy was electric. Like something we'd only seen on television and in the movies, but this time, the cameras were trained on us. Fox was decked out in pearls from her head to her feet, designed by Esé Azénabor and Lillian Shalom. Rob was draped in an onyx, stone-laced tuxedo—a Don Morphy original. And while our smiles were illuminated with gratitude and triumph, we also knew that Garrett Bradley's eighty-one-minute, mesmerizing portrait of our time together and apart was only a snapshot of our purpose as Fox and Rob. One unit. One voice. One name. Sure, it was certainly a full circle moment to be in that space. Only three years had passed since Rob was warehoused on 18,000 sprawling acres of swampy farmland at America's bloodiest penitentiary, Angola Maximum Security Prison. The fact that we were there—not in a jail cell, not struggling to put our family together—was proof that we'd won, even before they read the envelope and announced that *My Octopus Teacher* had taken the category.

We had already won.

Especially when you consider that our story had taken center stage during what some may characterize as the most electrifying social justice movement of our time.

However, there was an undeniable tension present that evening as well. Our joy lived alongside the awareness that, while our documentary had been nominated and our family was finally thriving, there was much that still had been lost. Much that we have to work daily to retain. And there is still so much more work that remains.

When Rob got home from prison, we jumped right into creating a work that has restored parole opportunities to over 3,000 incarcerated families in Louisiana who thought they'd never get a chance at freedom. We started Rich Family Ministries in our efforts to change lives and laws through love, and Participatory Defense Movement NOLA (PDMNOLA) was our first initiative—it is one of forty hubs nationwide. Through this national organizational model, we work with justice-involved citizens to reduce harm. We measure our success by the number of years behind bars that we save an individual from, as opposed to the number of years they may have to serve in prison.

And of course, there is Ontario, our beloved nephew who was sent to prison alongside Rob. Nothing else we do would matter if we could not make good on our promise to his parents, Rob's sister in particular, to bring him home. We'd started working on his case immediately upon Rob's release, and what a blessing it was to bring his mother and father down to Louisiana, put them up in a hotel, and handle all the Parole Board proceedings. The 20/45 geriatric parole law didn't work out for Rob, but it most certainly did for Ontario and more than 3,000 others who were now eligible due to the enactment of ACT 122. On February 18, 2022, Ontario was granted parole. And on June 8, 2022, he walked out of David Wade Correctional Institute a free man.

This is the work we will continue to do until our last breaths. This is what God has called us to do. Family by family, we will stand in the gap for those who have been crushed by a system that is sadly functioning the way it is designed to do. To date, we have saved more than 10,000 years across this country, with PDMNOLA representing more than 2,000 years of that time saved. And with 2.3 million families still languishing in our nation's prisons, the work continues!

Our ultimate goal is to share the power of God's grace, redemption, and radical love with the world through the facilitation of justice for the marginalized. In the words of Jesus fulfilling the prophecy of Isaiah, we want to "set the oppressed free" (Luke 4:18). This work isn't easy at all. It takes its toll. But whenever we look into each other's eyes and remember the love journey we've been on; when we watch all six of our sons do amazing and marvelous things in this world; when we are able to hold the hands of another mother, wife, brother, or uncle and tell them their family member is coming home, it's all worth it. Our fight has not been in vain. And through it all, the love of God has held us together. And it always will.

ACKNOWLEDGMENTS

To God be the glory!

At the conclusion of writing this book, we celebrated our twenty-fifth wedding anniversary on April 24, 2022. Our constant prayer is that our love continues to be a light in the world.

We are most humbled and elated to acknowledge each person on this list, as we are in some way deeply indebted to you for your specific impact on our story.

To Tracey Michae'l Lewis-Giggetts, our literary midwife: because of your spiritual gifts, we were able to birth what we believe will be a literary work for the ages.

To our *TIME* documentary family, the incomparable Garrett Bradley, the *New York Times*, the "creative genius" of Davis Guggenheim (Frank was right!), Concordia, and Amazon Studios: thank you for keeping your promise to tell the Richardson Family story as far and as wide as possible.

To Jeffrey Katzenburg for the introduction to one of the greatest entertainment attorneys of all time, Nina Shaw, whose legal acumen and towering advice has been the gust of wind beneath our wings.

To our agent, Cait Hoyt-Walden of Creative Artists Agency for believing that there was so much more to this story that needed to be told.

To our editor, Stephanie Duncan Smith, and the whole Baker Books team: thank you for recognizing our faith walk and giving us a home to amplify our message.

To Kenya Barris for hosting the black-ish dinner of a lifetime in honor of our family. We love you.

To The Game, a true Ambassador, for serving as a gateway, opening up your home and your heart, and for encouraging us to "write." What a welcome! Thanks, family.

To our play cousins Lena Waithe, Aisha Hinds, and Kacie Anderson for finding value in our story and our work.

To Shaka Senghor: thank you for penning *Writing My Wrongs: Life, Death, and Redemption in an American Prison* and being an inspiration for what is possible when we are willing to tell our stories.

Thank you so much to our aunt, uncle, and play cousin, Erykah Badu, Anthony Anderson, and Jessie Williams. We are extremely grateful to each of you for lending your social equity to the expansion of our story, allowing us to amplify the stories of the 2.3 million families still fighting.

To President Barack Obama and Bill Gates for sharing our story on your platforms. Drinks on us when we see you!

To the Ronald S. Haley Jr. law firm and Jim Craig of The Roderick and Solange MacArthur Justice Center: thank you for your grit and legal representation.

To our PDMNOLA family and cofounder Lisa Ellis: we are so grateful to you for supporting the work of bringing those closest to the pain closer to the power. A special thank you to SV-Debug (founders of PDM, Raj and Charrise Jayadev) for creating the model of participatory defense. And to Public Welfare Foundation for seeing the vision.

To Amy Povah for bearing witness to us that clemency is possible. Also, thank you to Louisiana Governor John Bel Edwards for exercising the power of his pen to restore our family.

To the National Council of Incarcerated and Formerly Incarcerated Women and Girls for unapologetically working to end the incarceration of women and girls. #FreeHer

Thank you to the Promise of Justice Initiative for your humanitarian efforts and unwavering support of PDMNOLA.

Thank you so much to the following organizations for the amazing work they do: Monique and Jim Brown's Amer-I-Can Foundation for Social Change, FFLIC, VOTE, The Power Coalition, and New Orleans Public Defenders office. We are forever indebted.

We appreciate the spiritual guidance we've received from Pastor Jerry and Julia Baldwin of New Living Word Ministries, the New Orleans Baptist Theological Seminary, Sula Spirit, and Mr. and Mrs. James Haywood Lester.

Finally, to the Autrey, Samuel, Richardson, and Stewart families—especially Fannie Mae and Otis Richardson, Peggy Autrey, and Isaiah Samuel—for teaching us the importance of family and the power in numbers. We are clearly stronger together.

We would be remiss if we did not acknowledge separately our amazing six sons: Mahlik, Remington, Lawrence, Freedom, Justus, and Robert II, who have been truly dynamic throughout this entire ordeal.

There are countless folks who served as a bridge over troubled water for our family. We are who and where we are because of your love and support. Thank you.

If you are reading these acknowledgments and don't see your name, please charge it to a lapse in our brains and not the immense love in our hearts.

Lastly, please remember this: when we fight, we win!

NOTES

Introduction

1. Josh Salman, Emily Le Coz, and Elizabeth Johnson, "Tough on Crime: Black defendants get longer sentences in Treasure Coast system," *Herald Tribune*, December 12, 2016, http://projects.heraldtribune.com/bias/bauer/.

2. Salman et al., "Tough on Crime," http://projects.heraldtribune.com/bias/bauer/.

3. "Demographic Differences in Sentencing," United States Sentencing Commission, November 14, 2017, https://www.ussc.gov/research/research-reports/demographic-differences-sentencing.

Chapter 2 For the Culture

1. *Set It Off*, directed by F. Gary Gray (Peak Films, 1996).

Chapter 3 Bond, Babies, and Conviction

1. Richard A. Serrano, "Withheld Evidence Can Give Convicts New Life," *Los Angeles Times*, May 29, 2001, https://www.latimes.com/archives/la-xpm-2001-may-29-mn-3771-story.html.

Chapter 4 Subject to the Systems That Shaped Us

1. Zora Neale Hurston, *Their Eyes Were Watching God*, Illini ed. (Champaign, IL: University of Illinois Press, 1978), 29.

Chapter 5 The Exception

1. Wayne W. Dyer, *You'll See It When You Believe It: The Way to Your Personal Transformation* (New York: William Morrow and Company, 2001), 127.
2. Les Brown, *Live Your Dreams* (New York: William Morrow and Company, 1994).
3. "#MLK: Street Sweeper," YouTube video, 3:30, posted by "The Martin Luther King, Jr. Center for Nonviolent Social Change," March 16, 2016, https://www.youtube.com/watch?v=cZiN8gMHs64.
4. "Top 15 Quotes to Remember by Booker T Washington," The Tom Joyner Foundation, accessed August 15, 2022, https://tomjoynerfounda tion.org/top-15-quotes-to-remember-by-booker-t-washington/.

Chapter 6 A Family Reunion

1. "2Pac – Picture Me Rollin'," YouTube video, 5:14, posted by "Seven Hip-Hop," May 22, 2020, https://www.youtube.com/watch?v=n8QurA BRsqE.
2. Paulo Coelho, *The Alchemist* (San Francisco: HarperOne, 2014), 22.
3. Rob read this in the Amer-I-Can program manual (page 14). While this is not publicly distributed, you can find out more information on their website: https://amer-i-cancommunity.partners/programs/.
4. *Earnie Miles Gospel Show* (Monroe: KNOE TV, 1979–2015).
5. "Media Matters: Finest Hour 136, Autumn 2007," International Churchill Society, July 4, 2013, https://winstonchurchill.org/publications /finest-hour/finest-hour-136/media-matters/.

Chapter 8 Heavy Is the Head That Wears the Crown

1. Henry Blackaby, Richard Blackaby, and Claude King, *Experiencing God (2021 Edition): Knowing and Doing the Will of God* (Nashville: B&H, 2021).
2. Jack Kornfield, *Buddha's Little Instruction Book* (New York: Bantam Books, 1994), 80.

Chapter 9 I Told the Storm

1. "Edutainment" is a clear platform and phrasing used often on KRS One in interviews and music.

Chapter 11 What You Won't Do for Love

1. Joy DeGruy Leary, *Post Traumatic Slave Syndrome: America's Legacy of Enduring Injury and Healing* (Milwaukie, OR: Uptone Press, 2005).

2. Bessel van der Kolk, *The Body Keeps the Score: Brain, Mind, and Body in the Healing of Trauma* (New York: Penguin Books, 2015).
3. La. Rev. Stat. § 15:574.4.2 (2018).
4. Judicial Review of Administrative Acts, La. Stat. tit. 15 § 1177 (2022).

Chapter 12 Mother of Invention

1. Fox Rich, *The One That Got Away* (LRND Publishings, 2009).

Chapter 13 Wind Beneath Our Wings

1. La. Rev. Stat. § 15:574.4.2 (2018).

Chapter 15 Victory Is Mine

1. Alvin Darling and Dorothy Norwood, "Victory is Mine," published by Peermusic/PEERTUNES LTD, Music Services, accessed August 15, 2022, https://musicservices.com/license/song/detail/204295.

Sibil Fox and **Robert Richardson** are a New Orleans–based couple who endured twenty-one years as an incarcerated family and whose story is told in the acclaimed, award-winning documentary *Time*. Together they have six sons and continue their advocacy for incarcerated families through the NOLA chapter of Participatory Defense Movement, an initiative of Rich Family Ministries, which they founded with the vision of "changing lives and laws through love" and dedicated to empowering families and marriages to thrive.